Perspectives on Game-Based Coaching

This book offers new perspectives on game-based coaching (GBC), one of the most important practices for session design and instructional delivery in sport coaching.

GBC emphasises the sport coach as educator and the development of 'thinking players', and this book demonstrates what that means in practice. It brings together leading and innovative thinkers and practitioners in coaching pedagogy, and aims to stimulate reflection by the reader on their own coaching practice. Reviewing recent theoretical developments and current research in GBC, the book provides in-depth examples on how research can be applied in practice, including the use of digital video games, immersive scenario-based coaching narratives, and the Game Sense approach as 'play with purpose'.

Representing the most up-to-date and engaging introduction to the theory and practice of GBC, this book is invaluable reading for all students of physical education and sport coaching, as well as practising coaches and coach educators.

Shane Pill is an Associate Professor in Physical Education and Sport, at Flinders University, Adelaide, Australia and a Life Member and Fellow of the Australian Council for Health, Physical Education and Recreation.

Contemporary Geographies of Leisure, Tourism and Mobility

Series Editor: C. Michael Hall, *Professor at the Department of Management, College of Business and Economics, University of Canterbury, Christchurch, New Zealand*

The aim of this series is to explore and communicate the intersections and relationships between leisure, tourism and human mobility within the social sciences.

It will incorporate both traditional and new perspectives on leisure and tourism from contemporary geography, e.g. notions of identity, representation and culture, while also providing for perspectives from cognate areas such as anthropology, cultural studies, gastronomy and food studies, marketing, policy studies and political economy, regional and urban planning, and sociology, within the development of an integrated field of leisure and tourism studies.

Also, increasingly, tourism and leisure are regarded as steps in a continuum of human mobility. Inclusion of mobility in the series offers the prospect to examine the relationship between tourism and migration, the sojourner, educational travel, and second home and retirement travel phenomena.

The series comprises two strands:

Contemporary Geographies of Leisure, Tourism and Mobility aims to address the needs of students and academics, and the titles will be published in hardback and paperback. Titles include:

The Moralisation of Tourism
Sun, Sand...and Saving the World?
Jim Butcher

The Ethics of Tourism Development
Mick Smith and Rosaleen Duffy

Routledge Studies in Contemporary Geographies of Leisure, Tourism and Mobility is a forum for innovative new research intended for research students and academics, and the titles will be available in hardback only. Titles include:

Living with Tourism
Negotiating Identities in a Turkish Village
Hazel Tucker

Tourism, Diasporas and Space
Edited by Tim Coles and Dallen J. Timothy

For more information about this series, please visit: www.routledge.com/Contemporary-Geographies-of-Leisure-Tourism-and-Mobility/book-series/SE0522

Perspectives on Game-Based Coaching

Edited by
Shane Pill

Routledge
Taylor & Francis Group

LONDON AND NEW YORK

First published 2021
by Routledge
2 Park Square, Milton Park, Abingdon, Oxon OX14 4RN

and by Routledge
605 Third Avenue, New York, NY 10017

First issued in paperback 2022

Routledge is an imprint of the Taylor & Francis Group, an informa business

© 2021 selection and editorial matter, Shane Pill; individual chapters, the contributors

The right of Shane Pill to be identified as the author of the editorial material, and of the authors for their individual chapters, has been asserted in accordance with sections 77 and 78 of the Copyright, Designs and Patents Act 1988.

All rights reserved. No part of this book may be reprinted or reproduced or utilised in any form or by any electronic, mechanical, or other means, now known or hereafter invented, including photocopying and recording, or in any information storage or retrieval system, without permission in writing from the publishers.

Trademark notice: Product or corporate names may be trademarks or registered trademarks, and are used only for identification and explanation without intent to infringe.

Publisher's Note
The publisher has gone to great lengths to ensure the quality of this reprint but points out that some imperfections in the original copies may be apparent.

British Library Cataloguing in Publication Data
A catalogue record for this book is available from the British Library

Library of Congress Cataloging-in-Publication Data
A catalog record has been requested for this book

ISBN: 978-0-367-61604-5 (pbk)
ISBN: 978-0-367-44047-3 (hbk)
ISBN: 978-1-003-00727-2 (ebk)

DOI: 10.4324/9781003007272

Typeset in Times New Roman
by Taylor & Francis Books

Contents

List of illustrations vii
List of contributors ix
Series editor's introduction xv
Introduction: game-based coaching xvii
SHANE PILL

1 The Game Sense approach as play with purpose 1
  SHANE PILL AND BRENDAN SUESEE

2 Digital video games as a game-based coaching tool 11
  AMY PRICE

3 Developing Thinking Players 23
  BARRIE GORDON

4 'Because we're here lad, and nobody else. Just us.': an existential–phenomenological perspective on game-based approaches 35
  RUAN JONES AND DAVID PIGGOTT

5 The practical application of immersive game-based narratives 45
  DAVID PIGGOTT AND RUAN JONES

6 Skilfulness on country: informal games and sports exposure 57
  JOHN ROBERT EVANS, RICHARD LIGHT AND GREG DOWNEY

7 Sport in physical education: evidencing learning from employing a game-based approach in badminton 67
  STEPHEN HARVEY AND MATTHEW POMEROY

8 Learning to be a game-changer 77
ADRIAN P. TURNER

9 Teaching players to think the game: beyond decision-making 86
CARLOS EDUARDO GONÇALVES, SERGE ÉLOI AND HUMBERTO M. CARVALHO

10 Exploring pedagogical tensions: providing practical examples for tennis coaches to navigate a shift to game-based coaching 96
MITCH HEWITT AND SHANE PILL

11 Exploring coach educators' experiences with developing game-based coaching 108
SHANE PILL AND DAVE REYNOLDS

12 Coaches' use of game-based approaches in team sports 117
DONNA O'CONNOR, PAUL LARKIN AND OLIVER HÖNER

Index 127

Illustrations

Figures

0.1.	A suggested lesson format from *Playground Games for Secondary Boys*	xviii
0.2.	Worthington's model of a continuum skill learning	xx
1.1.	The Game Sense as approach as non-linear pedagogy	2
1.2.	Mosston and Ashworth's Spectrum of Teaching Styles and the degree of teacher (coach) and student (player) decision-making	5
2.1.	Using a Digital Video Games approach for cricket	18
2.2.	Using a Digital Video Games approach for basketball	19
3.1.	Warmup activity one	27
3.2.	Activity three	29
3.3.	Activity four	31
5.1.	A game model of cricket	48
5.2.	A game model of basketball	54
10.1.	Groundstroke Scramble	99
10.2.	The CHANGE IT formula	102
10.3.	Jackpot – an activity for the 'Practice' element of the Game Sense approach as play with purpose	104

Tables

2.1.	Metacognitive game skills with examples from game two contrasting game categories	15
2.2.	Pedagogical principles for a Digital Video Games Approach	16
5.1.	A simplified model of invasion games	46
7.1.	Badminton middle school block plan outline using a Clinic Game-Day Model	69

7.2.	IMI questions	72
7.3.	Pre-post test team sport assessment procedure scores	73

Boxes

Rule to introduce	28
Rule to introduce	30
Rules to introduce	33

Contributors

Humberto M. Carvalho (PhD) is an Assistant Professor: Physical Education and Sport, at the Federal University of Santa Catarina, Brazil. Humberto's research is in youth sports, including athlete/coach development, and data analysis. Humberto began coaching in 2002. He has coached from U12-to-adult in basketball and continues his activity as a basketball coach. Humberto has worked with the Portuguese Basketball Federation, Portuguese Cycling Federation in Portugal, and the Basketball Federation of Santa Catarina in Brazil coach education, research or resource development.

Greg Downey is Professor of Anthropology at Macquarie University in Sydney. He is author of *Learning Capoeira: Lessons in Cunning from an Afro-Brazilian Art* (Oxford, 2005) and editor with Daniel Lende of *The Encultured Brain: An Introduction to Neuroanthropology* (MIT Press, 2012). Greg trained in cultural anthropology at the University of Chicago, working primarily in Brazil and the United States before moving to Australia. His principal research interests are in sports, dance, the senses, and skill acquisition, where he tries to bring together research from anthropology and the brain sciences with evolutionary theory, neuropsychology, and sports science. Greg is currently the Editor of *Ethos*, the journal of the Society for Psychological Anthropology.

Serge Éloi is a senior lecturer. In France, it means that he works in teaching and researching in equal proportion. Serge's research follows two paths: the first is performance analysis, including video analysis of performance, and the understanding of the relationship with the adversary. The second focuses on understanding the processes of instrumental genesis, starting from Vygotski's instrumental theory. Serge had a double career for a long time as a volleyball coach. His high-level experience began in 1996 with the French team. He oversaw statistics and game plans, then coached as an assistant coach (PSG VB, Poitiers, Paris VB), and then as Head Coach (Rennes, Saint Jean de Bray, Paris Saint Cloud).

John Robert Evans (PhD) is a Professor in the School of Sport, Exercise and Rehabilitation, University of Technology, Sydney. He has extensive experience in Aboriginal and Torres Strait Islander physical activity and sport research across both qualitative and quantitative disciplines. John has built an academic career, which has blended personal experience from the sport and physical activity industry with a professional career in the academy. John is recognised as a leading academic in the areas of Indigenous sport sociology, Indigenous sport and physical activity studies, pedagogy and coaching. He is one of a small number of Indigenous academics with the skills that can traverse both qualitative and quantitative methodologies and incorporate an Indigenous standpoint. His expertise has been sort by several national sporting organisations, including Netball Australia, National Rugby League, and the Australian Rugby Union.

Carlos E. Gonçalves (PhD) is an Assistant Professor: Physical Education and Sport, at the University of Coimbra, Portugal. Carlos's research is in youth sports, focusing on athlete/coach development, with a critical stance towards talent identification models and organisational environments. Carlos coached Basketball at professional and youth elite level, namely the Portuguese U18 and U20 national teams. Carlos has worked with the Portuguese Basketball, Cycling, Canoeing, Swimming and Hockey Federations, in coach education programs and research on athlete development.

Barrie Gordon (PhD) is an Associate Professor in physical education pedagogy at Victoria University of Wellington, New Zealand. Barrie's research is in physical education and sport-based youth development, with a specific interest in the Teaching Personal and Social Responsibility (TPSR) model. He is a strong advocate for increasing the emphasis on the youth development aspect of sport coaching. Barrie has received a Fulbright senior scholar award (2012) to study a sport-based youth development program for boys at risk in Illinois. He is a Fellow of Physical Education New Zealand.

Stephen Harvey (PhD) is Professor of Recreation and Sports Pedagogy at Ohio University, USA. Stephen is a prominent figure in research on game-based coaching (GBA). He was recently awarded the Society of Health and Physical Educators of America Curriculum and Instruction Award in 2019 in recognition of his research in this area. He is an international field hockey coach and currently coaches at a local soccer club. Stephen has led coach development sessions for numerous organisations, including USA Field Hockey and the United States Olympic Committee (USOC) in its National Team Coach Leadership and Development Program. Stephen is an accredited ICCE Coach Developer through his participation in the NSSU Coach Developer Academy.

Mitch Hewitt (PhD) has worked as a tennis coach, HPE teacher, and currently works for Tennis Australia in coach education. He completed his PhD in 2015 using the Spectrum to investigate coaching styles in tennis. He is the author of numerous articles on teaching styles and tennis. He holds an adjunct position at the University of Southern Queensland, and he has developed partnerships for the delivery of tennis programs with more than 20 universities in Australia.

Oliver Höner (PhD) is Professor of Sport Psychology and Research Methods at Eberhard Karls University of Tübingen (Germany). His main research interests include cognitive-perceptual and decision-making skills in sport games, talent identification and athlete development, sports coaching, and the evaluation of interventions in Physical Education. Oliver is the head of the scientific support of the talent development program in German football and the Sport Psychology Services for the VfB Stuttgart's professional youth academy. Oliver works for several committees with the German Football Association and the German Sport Federation. He has a UEFA A-Licence as a football coach and is currently vice president of the Association of German Football Coaches ('Bund Deutscher Fußballlehrer').

Ruan Jones (MSc PGCE FHEA) is a Senior Lecturer in Physical Education at Leeds Beckett University, West Yorkshire, UK. Ruan's research utilises phenomenological perspectives to explore the lived experiences of young people within physical education and sport settings. Ruan began coaching in 1994 when he started his secondary school teaching career. He has coached girls (U15 & U18) and boys (U18) age group county rugby union in Kent and North Yorkshire and was master in-charge of rugby union and athletics at several secondary schools during his teaching career.

Paul Larkin (PhD) is a Research Associate in the Institute for Health and Sport at Victoria University (Melbourne) and the Senior Sports

Scientist at Maribyrnong Sports Academy (Melbourne). Paul's research is in talent identification and development, coach education, and perceptual-cognitive skill development. At Maribyrnong Sports Academy, Paul supports athlete-performance monitoring, talent-identification processes, coach evaluation, and coaches' facilitation of athlete learning. He has worked with the Australian Football League; Football Federation Australia; and the Professional Footballer's Association (Soccer).

Richard Light (PhD) is a Professor at The University of Canterbury in New Zealand. He is a leading figure in the development of athlete-centred coaching with a focus on Game Sense and Positive Pedagogy. His coaching includes high performance sport in rugby in Japan and martial art where he coached several Australian national champions in kickboxing and karate. He has also coached children and young people across a range of sports in schools and community-based sport clubs in Australia, coached rugby in a Japanese high school and led tours of Australia by a Japanese university and two high school rugby teams. Richard has published over 200 outputs and 10 research books on sport over two decades as an academic.

Donna O'Connor (PhD) is a Professor of Sports Coaching and the course coordinator of the sports coaching program and HPE degree at the University of Sydney. Donna researches the effectiveness of sports coaching practices and the experiences of athletes and coaches in both youth and high performance contexts. A former strength and conditioning coach with the North Queensland Cowboys and Australian Women's basketball team, she consults with various sporting organisations, teams and schools. Donna is currently a member of the NRL research board, the World Congress Science and Football Steering Committee, and the International Council for Coaching Excellence Research Committee. Donna is a recipient of several teaching awards including a Carrick Citation for Outstanding Contributions to Student Learning and the University's Vice Chancellor's award for outstanding teaching.

David Piggott (PhD) is Head of Research at the English Football Association and a Senior Lecturer at Leeds Beckett University in the UK. David's research spans coaching, coach education, talent development, performance psychology and research methodology. David began coaching basketball in 1997 and has coached at all levels in the UK, from grassroots to professional. David is also an experienced coach developer and has evaluated world-leading programmes for UEFA, the Premier League and UK Sport. Most recently, David has delivered post-graduate coach education programmes for the English FA's professional game team.

Shane Pill (PhD) is an Associate Professor: Physical Education and Sport, at Flinders University, Adelaide, Australia. He is a Life Member and Fellow of the Australian Council for Health, Physical Education and Recreation. Shane researches in physical education, sport coaching, and coach development/education. Shane began coaching in 1988, coaching from U8-to-adult in multiple sports: Australian football (AFL), football (soccer), touch football, rugby union, athletics-sprinting, swimming, triathlon, basketball, cricket, volleyball. Shane was twice nominated for the Australian Football Coaches Association (WA) Coach of the Year award (1993, 1994), and in 2013 he was awarded the SANFL Coach Award for services to coach education. Shane has worked with Tennis Australia, Cricket Australia, the AFL, NRL, Australian Rugby, SANFL, WAFL, SASI, and Australian Lacrosse on coach education, research, or resource development.

Matthew Pomeroy has been teaching health and physical education since 2004 in Merton, WI. He has been a contributor to the PHYSEDagogy website since 2013 which includes writing blog posts and organising multiple online conferences. Matt is serving as a chair of the professional development committee for SHAPE America's Midwest District and volunteers on the Board of Directors with Wisconsin Health and Physical Education Organisation. Matt created and produced The SHAPE America Podcast. He strongly believes in the continual development of educators to keep students motivated and engaged in physical education, so students will be fit for life!

Amy Price is Women's National Coach Developer for the English Football Association, and a PhD student at University of Edinburgh. Amy's research is in sport coaching, and specifically the role of metacognition for team sport players. Amy began coaching in 2003 and is a UEFA A licensed coach. She has coached soccer in a range of contexts, such as grassroots, talent and professional pathways with male and female teams. Amy was Programme Director for Sport Education (BA, Hons) at St Mary's University (England), and began her journey in coach education and development for the English FA in 2015. Amy has worked with England Rugby Union,

English Cricket Board, and a range of English independent schools on her PhD research.

Dave Reynolds is the State Coaching Manager at the South Australian National Football League (SANFL), having been employed at SANFL since 2009. Dave is an AFL Level 3 High Performance Accredited coach currently coaching with the U16 Male SA State Team. He has 20 years coaching experience having coached both male and female teams in Australian football (AFL) from U8s through to adults at community, college, state league and national level. His position at SANFL focuses strongly on providing coach development to Australian football (AFL) coaches at all levels across South Australia.

Brendan SueSee (PhD) is a lecturer at the University of Southern QLD. His research interests include pedagogy, teaching styles, Mosston & Ashworth's Spectrum, curriculum and syllabus documents. In the last 4 years since becoming a 'pracademic' he has published over 14 articles and book chapters and presented extensively at conferences. In 2020 he co-edited and co-authored The Spectrum of Teaching Styles in Physical Education. Brendan was a high school HPE, PE, Health Education, Geography and History teacher for 20 years. Brendan held positions such as Head of Department, year co-ordinator, acting Deputy Principal, Sports Master and subject co-ordinator. He continues to coach touch football, cricket, netball and baseball at junior club level.

Adrian P. Turner (PhD) is an Associate Professor of Sport Pedagogy and Coaching at Bowling Green State University in Ohio, USA. Adrian's scholarship focuses on tactical approaches to teaching games and he has published and presented nationally and internationally on Teaching Games for Understanding, providing empirical support as well as practical application of the model to coaching practices in various sports including: cricket, field hockey, lacrosse (modified), rugby, soccer, and team handball. Adrian has conducted numerous in-service workshops on games teaching for physical educators and coaches and continues to invoke a game-based approach during his soccer coaching at the grass roots level. In 2020 he was invited to serve as the Director of Coaching for the Bowling Green Soccer Club.

Series editor's introduction

This book offers a fantastic focus on games-based coaching. It packs a series of powerful chapters into a small space and I thoroughly enjoyed reading each of the bite-sized morsels of knowledge and understanding crammed into each of the thirteen chapters. In fact, I enjoyed it so much I read it from cover to cover in an afternoon.

When I first placed my feet on the road towards pedagogical change, I was crying out for practical examples of what I might do to replace my 'skills and drills' 'do as I do' approach to teaching and coaching. Furthermore, and as Rink (2001) indicated, I didn't just 'want to know simply that something works – [I] want[ed] to know why it works' (p. 23). Truth be told Griffin, Mitchell and Oslin (1997) became my guides through games-based approaches (although they never knew it). However, while their book(s) were brimming with practical examples there was little in the way of theory and little in the way of variation. What Shane Pill has achieved in this edited collection is praxis i.e. research-informed practice, and I thank and commend him (and each chapter author) on realising the aspiration I had for this series of books when I first discussed it with Simon Whitmore at Routledge.

Since leaving secondary education and entering university teaching and teacher education I have continually sought to facilitate practitioner understanding of research. Through different avenues I've tried to share and translate research for colleagues in schools and sports clubs who are short on time and separated from research by a paywall. This book carries the baton of that idea forwards and I hope you enjoy reading it (and using it) as much as I did/will.

Ash Casey, 22 April 2020

References

Griffin, L. L., Mitchell, S. A. & Oslin, J. L. (1997). *Teaching sport concepts and skills: A tactical games approach*. Champaign, IL: Human Kinetics.

Rink, J. E. (2001). Investigating the assumptions of pedagogy. *Journal of Teaching in Physical Education*, 20, 112–128.

Introduction
Game-based coaching

Shane Pill

In April 2015, after posting a manuscript on the Game Sense approach (ASC; Australian Sports Commission, 1996) on the Academia.edu site I was running at the time, I received a message inquiring if in addition to the work of Allen Wade and Eric Worthington, had I looked at the work of Charles Hughes, Walter Winterbottom, Ron Greenwood, Eric Batty, Trevor Brooking and Harry Redknapp. Since I started publishing on the Game Sense coaching approach, I have received many emails like this one asking 'have I looked at …', from coaches who suggest books and readings to find similar ideas to the game-based approach to teaching for understanding and developing thinking players that preceded the Game Sense approach.

Game-based approaches have arguably been recognised in coaching since the late 1960s. One of my favourite books is Grehaigne, Richard and Griffin's (2005) *Teaching and Learning Team Sports and Games*, and in it they reference the earlier work of Deleplace and Mahlo. The work of Deleplace (1966, 1972, 1979), Wade (1967), Mahlo (1969) and Worthington (1974) seem to recognise purposeful game play in developing playing ability. Thus, coaching practice deliberately for tactical intelligence (Deleplace, 1979) and developing thinking players (Australian Sports Commission, 1996) is not a new concept. At its core, game-based coaching is a paradigm shift from over reliance on highly directive coaching for player replication of what is prescribed by the coach – sport as techniques to be drilled by direct instruction – to the 'sport coach as educator' (Jones, 2006) developing 'thinking players'. However, game-based coaching is still poorly understood at many levels of coaching.

Game-based approaches prompt player thinking

Wade's (1967) *The FA Guide to Training and Coaching* presented the concept that coaches 'must provoke thought and enquiry among their

Section	Activity
A	Team Game
B	Revision of known work
C	Teaching of new work
D	Team Game

Figure 0.1 A suggested lesson format from *Playground Games for Secondary Boys*.
Source: Williams and Willee (1954, p. 6)

players' (p. vii). The game of football (soccer) is set out as three phases: attack, defence, preparation or midfield play. From the three phases principles of play Wade suggested a system of play ('a recognizable pattern of play resulting from the use of certain players in fairly clearly defined functions on the field'; Wade, 1967, p. 43) is enabled and tactical considerations developed. The ten principles of play outlined by Wade are: Depth in attack; Depth in defence; Penetration in defence; Delay in defence; Concentration in defence; Width in attack; Mobility in attack; Balance in defence; Control and restraint in defence; and Improvisation in attack.

Wade (1967) outlined a practice schedule:

- Match Practice – developing systems of play
- Small sided games – developing principles of play and tactical possibilities
- Functional training: phase practice – developing understanding between small groups of players
- Tactical practice – developing set plays

Wade (1967) suggested that individual technique through repetitive practice occur outside of the training from practice, or individual technical work may occur in the warm-up phase prior to the practice commencing. According to Wade, decision-making is 'probably the most important single factor in developing skill at the game. It follows therefore, that practice situations must include these elements' (p. 181). It is of 'considerable importance that a player should understand why a certain aspect of play is necessary as opposed to merely being shown how it is achieved' (p. 185). Therefore, 'all coaching should begin with some form of realistic competitive situation' (p. 186).

Worthington's (1974) *Teaching Soccer Skills* sets out a 'principles of play' coaching approach. 'With a practical understanding of the principles of play it is again a normal feature for such players to be able to fit into any system of play or formation' (p. 54). The following principles of play are contained in the approach:

- Delay in defence: first defender
- Depth in defence: second defender
- Concentration and balance in defence: the third defender
- Penetration in attack: the first attacker
- Depth and width in attack: the second attacker
- Mobility in attack: the third attacker

Worthington suggested that 'initially, the coach should do no more than organise the players to play' (1974, p. 160). This led into one of the key coaching tenets of the text, Realism:
"To effect the best transfer from what is done in training session, practices should be used which are similar to those that players face in the game ... the more realistic a practice the better the transfer will be" (Worthington, 1974, p. 161).

Another of the pedagogical tenets of Worthington's Principles of Play approach is the concept of 'freeze replay'. This is where 'the players must stop precisely where they are at the time the coach demands that they stop' (Worthington, 1974, p. 172). The coach then uses this real situation as a 'living tactical board to show the players what they are doing' (ibid., p. 172). The way Worthington described the use of this pedagogy, the coach goes into observation of the game play knowing what game moment they are looking for, as they have decided going into practice what idea they wish to develop with the players.

Worthington set out a continuum of skill practice, which I find a useful reference when thinking about the purpose of an activity and the 'realism' of activities when coaching. If a number is assigned to the levels, a coach can rate the 'realism' load of the practice session.

Worthington called the process of deliberate game design 'conditioned games', which are different to games where players can respond 'freely' as the coach intentionally restricts the game to change the condition of practice. Conditioned games are purposefully changed in the following ways:

- vary the number of players;
- change the pitch shape or size;
- change the method of scoring;
- change the laws of the game;
- demand the players respond in a set way during play.

Figure 0.2 Worthington's model of a continuum skill learning.
Source: Worthington (1974, p. 154)

Game-based coaching and systems of play

> Someone brings up the fact that Clarkson is going to tactically have an impact on this game – you haven't watched the way I've coached for 14 years. We're a system-based side and that's why Richmond are so strong at the moment. They're system-based – every side that's won a premiership is system-based.
> (Alistair Clarkson, 4-time AFL Premiership Coach, 7 September 2018)

Grehaigne and colleagues provided insight into game-based coaching and systems of play. Grehaigne and Godbout (1995) defined strategy as the elements discussed in advance in order that a team organise itself, while tactics are an in the moment of the game adaptation of player to the opposition. In describing games as an opposition relationship in which two teams or players coordinate their actions, they consider three 'indissociable' characteristics:

- a group of players (or a player: e.g. tennis) confronts another group of players (or player) fighting for, or exchanging possession, of an object (which Grehaigne and colleagues described as a *rapport of strength*; Grehaigne & Godbout, 1995; Grehaigne, Godbout & Bouthier, 2011);
- players have a choice of motor skills; and
- the game involves individual and collective strategies.

From a system-based perspective, the game has many dynamically interacting elements capable of rich and varied patterns. The implications for practice schedules are that the simple application of schemes of play during training are not sufficient and players need heuristics (a 'rule of thumb' or a 'good guide') to help them quickly solve the problems that present from the way attack and defence configurations evolve (Grehaigne, Bouthier & David, 1997). A conclusion is that players need to pay attention to the shifts in configurations of play in order to better understand how the play is evolving. To assist players develop this capacity, novice players should be guided with heuristics that provide them with a reference to probable indicators of the evolution of the situation of play, so that over time they learn to ignore the parameters that are not pertinent in making appropriate decisions. Grehaigne and colleagues proposed practice to develop this understanding comprise action settings where the players engage in the actual game, or a form of the game, observation settings where players observe peers, usually with reference to performance criteria, and a debate of ideas settings following play action, during which there is an exchange of facts or ideas based on observation and participation in the activity (Grehaigne, Godbout & Bouthier, 2001).

Explanations for skill developing from game-based coaching

Game-based approaches represent a shift from a behaviourist orientation to sport coaching where the focus is on replicating the coach instructions and demonstrations. The previous examples in this introduction could be viewed as a move to a more 'cognitive orientation' to player learning. From a cognitive lens on player behaviour during a game, what is observed as a movement response to the demands of the moment of play is a tactical action (Mahlo, 1974 in Grehaigne et al., 2005). Hopper's (2003) '4r's: read, respond, react recover' explanation of game behaviour and Mahlo's explanation of skilled behaviour as occurring as the player has (1) perceived and analysed the moment, (2) resolved a mental solution to the problem of the moment, and (3) produced a motor skill solution (Grehaigne et al., 2005), are examples of cognitive explanations for skilled performance. Scott (2004) also provided a cognitive explanation of skill consisting of the interaction between three components – motor behaviour, movement mechanics and neural control. Similarly, Patterson and Lee's (2013) 3Bs model – brain, biomechanics and behaviour. In the 3Bs model, the process of movement skill commences with cognition of the moment, followed by the brain organising a movement plan for the body to achieve the goal decided as the outcome of the movement. How well the player delivers the movement plan is a function of biomechanics.

> Ashleigh Barty likens a tennis match to a slightly more energetic game of chess.
>
> (Herman, 2019)

From a cognitive perspective, a game-based approach might also be considered thus: player learning occurs by testing the player's cognitive frameworks. This necessarily requires participation in game play. The coach conditions the game as an 'advanced organiser' of information deliberately to assist players to retrieve and then to learn information (advanced organiser is a name for a pedagogical tool that bridges a gap between what a learner currently knows and what is planned for the learner to know: Ausubel, 2000). Practice games are therefore designed with purpose: to allow for the contextual emergence of a cognising moment; to capture the meaning of that moment; and then inserting that meaning back into the context. The 'principles of play' become an information organiser and a 'unifying concept' for shared meaning.

Learning to play a sport can thus be considered an emergent process from an adaptive and self-organising response by the player arising from repeated engagement within a complex structure, called a game (Hopper, 2011). The role of a coach is to assist this process.

Another explanation for skilful game behaviour is provided by the lens of ecological modelling leading to a constraints approach to practice design (Renshaw, Davids & Savelsbergh, 2010). Ecological modelling of games as dynamic systems leads to consideration of the role of perception of environmental, task and performer constraints in directing players' action. Direct perception is often suggested with the player mapping the dynamics of the moment as patterns of play resulting in functionally preferred movement models constructed 'in the moment' by the player to meet the situated dynamics of the moment. To explain effective transfer from practice to the performance context, ecological modelling includes the concept of representative task design for the emergence of skills under constraints (Pinder, Renshaw, Headrick & Davids, 2014). Representative design of the practice environment leads to the same emerging patterns of movement organisation and performance outcomes in practice as the game.

The theory of affordances is a conceptual foundation of ecological modelling of perception and action in sport leading to a constraints-led approach to game-based coaching (Rankin, Pill & Magias, 2018). Affordances are properties in the environment that indicate possibilities for action (Turvey, 1992). If we assume a player to be a set of capabilities, then there is the possibility of a niche set of affordances for a player based on the player's functional ability to perceive and act. For example, two players may be in the same moment of action during play, but their set of affordances do not overlap and the player with greater functional ability will have a competitive performance advantage. Thus, at any given moment in a game a player is in an environment that provides some affordances and not others. There is then a dynamic between the player and the playing environment (Rankin et al., 2018). The implication for coaching practice is to design settings to prepare players to perform in this dynamic – in other words, in the game (Pill, 2014). Information from practice will transfer to the game if the contexts of practice and the game overlap in a meaningful way: that is, the contexts share information. In this perspective, practice must be an environment that represents the same affordances and therefore the same information as the game, at a relevant complexity for the challenge points of the players (Rankin et al., 2018).

Game-based coaching: many variations

There now exists a suite of game-based approaches for sport coaching that focus on the complementarity of technical and technical game development. In addition to those outlined already in this chapter, Teaching Games for Understanding (Bunker & Thorpe, 1982), Designer games (Charlesworth, 1994), Game Sense (Australian Sports Commission, 1996), Tactical Games (Griffin, Mitchell & Oslin, 1997), Play Practice (Launder, 2001), Game Intelligence (Wein, 2004), Constraints-led (Davids, Button & Bennett, 2008), Play with Purpose (Pill, 2012), and Game Insight (Weeldenburg, Zondag & de Kok, 2016) are some of the nuanced variations of game-based coaching. Sometimes, sports develop their own versions or labels for what is essential still one of the game-based approaches established in the literature. As an example, the US Soccer play-practice-play approach (US Soccer, 2018) is very similar to the game-practice-game approach illustrated in Tactical Games (Griffin et al., 1997). Despite the plethora of variations, in general game-based approaches involve playing the game or a game form as the central organisational feature of the coaching session. The game or game form is conditioned (modified, constrained or adapted – the language depending on your epistemological lens) for the players' ability and to emphasise a game feature in order to develop player understanding and decision-making as a key outcome of the session (Australian Sports Commission, 1996; Breed & Spittle, 2011).

Game-based coaching is positioned centrally in athlete-centred coaching (Kidman, Hadfield & Thorpe, 2005; Pill, 2018). This is not surprising as the nature of game-based coaching lends itself to the encouragement of players participation in decision-making and problem-solving in a shared approach to knowledge and its transmission, and ultimately the positioning of the player as responsible for their game development as a self-directed, self-responsible, learner.

Chapter summaries

In Chapter 1, Pill and SueSee detail pedagogical concepts to clarify the instructional decision-making associated with practice design of game-based coaching sessions. As they work in Australia, they use the Game Sense approach (Australian Sports Commission, 1996) to illustrate game-based coaching as a cluster of teaching styles. Also using a pedagogical lens, in Chapter 2 Price adopts an innovative attitude to game-based coaching using insights from digital game design theory. Price pays particular attention to the role of conditional knowledge and its relationship to thinking strategically in the quest to outwit the opposition, suggesting a meta-cognitive view of game-based coaching. In Chapter 3, Gordon applies the Teaching Games for Understanding (TGfU) model (Bunker & Thorpe, 1982) to coaching as Developing Thinking Players (DTP). DTP is distinct in emphasis on two areas: developing tactical understanding and good decision-making. The chapter explains how the two form the framework from which a wider game understanding develops.

Jones and Piggott provide two chapters, Chapter 4 and 5 that first outline a theory for Immersive Scenario-based Coaching Narratives (ISN) and then illustrate the value and application of ISNs in three different sports: basketball, football (soccer) and cricket. ISNs propose to place athletes into counter-factual conditioned situations to provide the scenario greater meaning and hence a greater stake in achieving success. Jones and Piggott argue that ISNs provide two ingredients often missing in game-based coaching: the central importance of contextual decision-making based on realistic risk assessment, and connection to the players' emotions and lived experiences.

Evans and colleagues report on a three-year ARC study which examined the pedagogical influences on elite Indigenous players in the Australian Football League (AFL) and the National Rugby League (NRL) in Chapter 6. They conclude that Indigenous players display a unique style characterised by high order decision making and athleticism, often developed in the absence of a directive approach from coaches as participation in sport occurs within a sociocultural context where sport is highly associated with local culture. Skilfulness is attached to participation in informal games and exposure to a range of sports in the sampling phase.

Chapter 7 discusses the application of game-based coaching ideas to sport teaching in physical education. Harvey and Pomeroy use badminton in primary/elementary school physical education to illustrate game-based coaching ideas and through their collaboration, demonstrate the value of academic-practitioner partnership as collaborative action research. Football (soccer) is used by Turner in Chapter 8 to examine the intricacy of coach interpretation of game-based coaching over the duration of a specific session. The pedagogical structure of the game-based soccer coaching scenario may be approximated to Light's (2013) description of Game Sense pedagogy.

Goncalves and colleagues present the idea of games as a pedagogical technology in Chapter 9. They suggest the need to explore the interactions between individual learners/athletes exposed and responding to the coaches' intervention, within the different learning environments to enable games to be a powerful tool to teach and learn sport. Goncalves and colleagues favour Vygotski's instrumental theory through the concepts of sign, conscience or experience, to provide the intellectual ground for the use of coaching artefacts and for the evaluation of their utility. In Chapter 10, Hewitt and Pill outline the tension between how coaches perceive their instructional practice and what they desire it to be, and then provide practical examples that will guide coaches to adopt a 'toolkit' that emphasises representative activities relevant to a game-based approach. Drawing on the concept of the sport coach as educator (Jones, 2006) and the idea of an 'everyday' philosophy of teaching developed by Green (1998, 2000, 2002), in Chapter 11, Pill and Reynolds create a dialogue between two coach educators who are also practicing coaches to explore an assumed acceptance of game-based coaching. They suggest that from their experience as coach developers, coaches often operate from an 'everyday' philosophy and pragmatic interpretation of game-based approaches and 'what works' for them, rather than employing a replication of the conceptualised instructional approach found in coaching and research literature.

Chapter 12 provides a coming together of the key ideas contained in the book. In this chapter, O'Connor and colleagues recognise that as an effective pedagogy, there is still a need for further understanding of coaches' perceptions of game-based approaches and how they are used for athlete development. The chapter considers why coaches use game-based approaches for athlete development and provides examples of the strategies used by coaches to incorporate a game-based approach into sessions. The chapter concludes with recommendations for both practitioners, in relation to how to incorporate game-based approaches into their practice sessions, and sport coaching and pedagogy researchers to further our understanding of the strengths and limitations of game-based approaches for athlete development.

Conclusion

This book is intended to engage undergraduate and postgraduate students in physical education and sport coaching, practicing coaches and coach educators. The contributions, taken together or individually, will provide insight, learning and opportunities to foster game-based coaching ideas. Each chapter will raise issues that can resonate with the sport practitioner and researcher. In this way, the chapters can assist practitioners to make sense of their own coaching, provide deeper insight into personal conceptualisations of the concept of game-based coaching, stimulate reflections on one's coaching or the coaching contexts they are involved in. This book both summarises current thinking, debates and practical considerations about game-based coaching as well as providing direction for further practical, pragmatic and research consideration of the concept and its precepts.

References

Ausubel, D. P. (2000). *The acquisition and retention of knowledge: A cognitive view*. Boston, MA: Kluwer.

Australian Sports Commission. (1996). *Game sense: Perceptions and actions*. Belconnen, ACT: Australian Sports Commission.

Breed, R. & Spittle, M. (2011). *Developing game sense through tactical learning: A resource for teachers and coaches*. Melbourne, Vic: Cambridge University Press.

Bunker, D. J. & Thorpe, R. D. (1982). A model for the teaching of games in Secondary Schools. *Bulletin of Physical Education*, 18(1), 5–8.

Charlesworth, R. (1994). Designer games. *Sport Coach* 17(4), 30–33.

Clarkson, A. (2018). Alastair Clarkson labels reporters a 'bunch of sheep'. Retrieved from www.news.com.au/sport/afl/alastair-clarkson-labels-reporters-a-bunch-of-sheep/news-story/388df18e846d1dfb7117e7516665a855.

Davids, K., Button, C. & Bennett, S. (2008). *Dynamics of skill acquisition: A constraints-led approach*. Champaign, IL: Human Kinetics.

Deleplace, R. (1966). *Le Rugby. Analyse technique et pédagogie*. Paris: Armand Colin Bourrelier.

Deleplace, R. (1972). *L'enseignement du rugby*. Paris: Colloque des cadres techniques de la FFR.

Deleplace, R. (1979). *Rugby de mouvement – rugby total*. Paris: Education Physique et Sports.
Green, K. (1998). Philosophies, ideologies and the practices of physical education. *Sport, ducation and Society*, 3(2), 125–143.
Green, K. (2000a). Exploring the everyday 'philosophies' of physical education teachers from a sociological perspective. *Sport, Education and Society*, 5(2), 109–129.
Green, K. (2002). Physical education teachers in theory figurations: A sociological analysis of everyday 'philosophies'. *Sport, Education and Society*, 7(1), 65–83.
Greenwood, R. (2019). Eddie's wonder goal shows practice makes perfect: Tex. *The Advertiser*, 24 April.
Grehaigne, J-F. & Godbout, P. (1995). Tactical knowledge in team sports from a constructivist and cognitivist perspective. *Quest*, 47, 490–505.
Grehaigne, J.-F., Bouthier, D. & David, B. (1997). Dynamics system analysis of opponent relationships in collective actions in soccer. *Journal of Sports Sciences*, 15, 137–149.
Grehaigne, J-F., Godbout, P. & Bouthier, D. (2001). The teaching and learning of decision making in team sports. *Quest*, 53, 59–76.
Grehaigne, J-F., Richard, J-F. & Griffin, L. (2005). *Teaching and learning team sports and games*. New York: Routledge.
Grehaigne, J-F., Godbout, P. & Bouthier, D. (2011). The foundations of tactics and strategy in team sports. *Journal of Teaching in Physical Education* 18(2), 159.
Griffin, L., Mitchell, S. & Oslin, J. (1997). *Teaching sports concepts and skills: A tactical games approach*. Champaign, IL: Human Kinetics.
Herman, M. (2019). Crafty Barty solving the clay court puzzle. Retrieved from www.thestar.com.my/sport/tennis/2019/06/06/crafty-barty-solving-the-clay-court-puzzle.
Hopper, T. (2003). Four Rs for tactical awareness: Applying game performance assessment in net/wall games. *Teaching Elementary Physical Education*, 14(2), 16–21.
Hopper, T. (2011). Game-as-teacher: Modification by adaptation in learning through game-play. *Asia-Pacific Journal of Health, Sport and Physical Education*, 2(2), 3–21.
Jones, R. (2006). *The sports coach as educator*. New York: Routledge.
Kidman, L., Hadfield, D. & Thorpe, R. (2005). *Athlete-centred coaching: Developing inspired and inspiring people*. Christchurch, NZ: Innovative Print Communications.
Launder, A. (2001). *Play practice: The games approach to teaching and coaching sports*. Champaign, IL: Human Kinetics.
Light, R. (2013). *Game sense: Pedagogy for performance, participation and enjoyment*. New York, NY: Routledge.
Mahlo F. (1969). *Acte tactique en jeu*. Paris: Vigot Freres.
Patterson, J. E. & Lee, T. D. (2013). Organizing practice: Effective practice is more than just reps. In D.Farrow, J.Baker & C. McMahon (eds), *Developing*

sport expertise: Researchers and coaches put theory into practice (pp. 132–153). New York: Routledge.
Pill, S. (2012). *Play with purpose: Developing game sense in AFL footballers.* Hindmarsh, SA: ACHPER Publications.
Pill, S. (2014). Informing game sense pedagogy with constraints-led theory for coaching in Australian football. *Sports Coaching Review*, 3(1), 46–62.
Pill, S. (2018). *Perspectives on athlete-centred coaching.* New York: Routledge.
Pinder, R. A., Renshaw, I., Headrick, J. & Davids, K. (2014). Skill acquisition and representative task design. In K. Davids, R. Hristovski, D. Araújo, N. Balagué Serre, C. Button & P. Passos (eds), *Routledge research in sport and exercise science: Complex systems in sport* (pp. 319–333). New York: Routledge.
Rankin, J., Pill, S. & Magias, T. (2018). Informing the coaching pedagogy of game modification in a game sense approach with affordance theory. *Ágora para la Educación Física y el Deporte*, 20(1), 68–89.
Renshaw, I., Davids, K. & Savelsbergh, G. P. (eds) (2010). *Motor learning in practice: A constraints-led approach.* New York: Routledge.
Scott, S. H. (2004). Optimal feedback control and the neural basis of volitional motor control. *Nature Reviews: Neuroscience*, 5, 534–536.
Turvey, M. (1992). Affordances and prospective control: An outline of the ontology. *Ecological Psychology*, 4(3), 173–187.
US Soccer. (2018). Play–practice–play. Retrieved from www.ussoccer.com/stories/2018/02/five-things-to-know-about-playpracticeplay.
Wade, A. (1967). *The FA guide to training and coaching.* London: Heinemann.
Wein, H. (2004). *Developing game intelligence in soccer.* Spring City, PA: Reedswain.
Williams, L. C. & Willee, A. W. (1954). *Playground games for secondary boys.* London: Blackie & Son Limited.
Weeldenburg, G., Zondag, E. & de Kok, F. (2016). *Spelinzicht: Een speler- en spelgecentreerde didactiek van spelsporten* [Game Insight: A learner and game-centred approach to teaching games]. Zeist, Nederland: Jan Luiting Fonds.
Worthington, E. (1974). *Teaching soccer skills.* UK: Lepus Books.

1 The Game Sense approach as play with purpose

Shane Pill and Brendan SueSee

In the late 1960s and into the 1970s game-based approaches to sport teaching and coaching emerged in scholarly literature and coaching books. Game-based pedagogical approaches for games and sport teaching have been distinguished by some authors through the more prominent emphasis on guided discovery teaching and player reflective thinking than what occurs in the more historically common sport-as-sport techniques approach, which is exemplified by a 'transmission' method of instruction (Kirk, 2010). In this chapter, we suggest that rather than be competing approaches, game-based approaches can be viewed as a 'toolkit' of instructional styles governed by a fundamental proposition – pedagogical decision making (SueSee, Pill & Edwards, 2016). We examine a game-based coaching episode and identify the decisions made between the coach and players using the Spectrum of Teaching Styles (Mosston & Ashworth, 2008). By doing this, we detail pedagogical concepts that clarify pedagogical decision making that take place when sport coaching is aimed across the 'discovery barrier' and into an intentionally designed coaching space to develop 'thinking players'. This explanation will highlight that game-based coaching is a sophisticated pedagogical endeavour.

Light (2013) suggested four pedagogical principles identify a game-based approach:

1   deliberate design of the game as a learning environment;
2   emphasising questioning to promote inquiry and interaction;
3   promoting inquiry through problem solving; and
4   a supportive environment.

It is the first of these pedagogical principles that we pick-up on in this chapter, because the use of small-sided and modified games is common in sport coaching, while the deliberate design of the game in our experience often gets lost in the understanding of game-based coaching. Furthermore, we focus on the principle of deliberate design as the concept of 'game first' rather than 'drill first' is also not a new or recent suggestion for the focus of practice sessions.

We work within the context of sport coaching in Australia, where the Game Sense approach (GSA; Australian Sports Commission, 1996) has been the preferred pedagogical expression for games teaching since the mid-1990s (den Duyn, 1997a, 1997b), and remains the pedagogical approach underpinning the Playing for Life Philosophy (Schembri, 2005) of Australian sport development (Sport Australia, 2019). Recently, the GSA has been positioned with the Sport Australia Physical Literacy Strategy (Sport Australia, 2020). A central component of the GSA is that games are adapted or modified for specific reasons (Australian Sports Commission, 1996). Pill (2007) suggested that a GSA would also be evident by the enacted structure of practice sessions. Whereas the typical sport coaching session has been linear, in the sense that it progresses in order from closed to open drills and then a game, a GSA sequence is more likely to be non-linear (Figure 1.1): game-play analysis through question and reflection; skill practice if necessary – return to a game.

The idea of development of 'thinking players' is synonymous with the Game Sense coaching approach (Australian Sports Commission, 1996). Because of a GSA focus on developing 'thinking players' a foregrounding of 'guided discovery' has been suggested. This arguably embraces a more cognitive orientation compared with the behaviourist orientation of command and directive instruction associated with a linear 'technical to tactical' coaching approach asking for replication of very specific movement models. However, it is also arguable that the

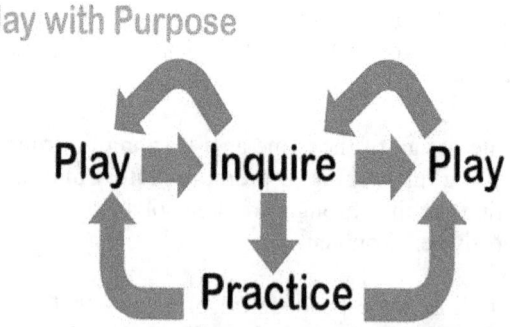

Figure 1.1 The Game Sense as approach as non-linear pedagogy.

enacted structure of a GSA session through game modifications is also consistent with tenets of skill learning associated with an ecological appreciation of the dynamics of sport learning (Breed & Spittle, 2011; Pill, 2014; Rankin, Pill & Magias, 2018).

Deliberate design for play with purpose

Game practice is a discriminating factor in performance attainment, and deliberate practice is recognised as a central component in the development of sport expertise (Hendry & Hodges, 2019). However, in training sessions dominated by drill type practice tasks information about how to act at practice is not the same as that encountered by the player in the competitive game. Transfer of learning from practice to the game day experience is therefore problematic (Pill, 2014), and indeed may be detrimental to game performance by narrowing perceptual attention (Memmert, 2015; Pill, 2016). We are not suggesting here that drills are bad or not to be used as a practice tool. Coaches have always used a range of pedagogies (Light, 2006), and there are times when it is necessary for direct instruction or a focus on technique (Light, 2004; Light, 2006), which we will elaborate upon in the next section of the paper. However, we suggest that the notion of directiveness in execution of a GSA relates to process directiveness. This is where the coach deliberately facilitates player technical and tactical skill complementarity by a focus on guiding discovery of game understanding to develop the 'thinking player' (Pill, 2012, 2015). However, time alone spent in game play is not necessarily enough to ensure positive changes in movement skill competency (Fischer et al., 2005; Hendry & Hodges, 2019). Learning and development do not necessarily occur with experience alone (Pill, 2017). Improvement occurs through deliberate effort (Hendry & Hodges, 2019), with the critical elements under control of the coach being planning, guidance, pedagogical choice, goal setting and feedback (Hattie & Yates, 2014).

We suggest that if the focus is developing 'thinking players' then deliberate practice in a GSA is a pattern of coach-athlete interaction purposefully directed to changing the quality of mental representations of performance. Through this type of practice, it is hypothesised that faster and more accurate performance decisions develop over time. The representative task design typical of this type of deliberate practice requires a coach who can provide a practice environment designed for learning, not just doing (Ericsson & Pool, 2016). In very simple terms, the GSA as play with purpose is deliberate practice as the environment of play is designed by the coach for player engagement in the specific purpose of improvement.

In using a GSA to deliberately condition game play, the pedagogy the coach employs to achieve play with purpose is game modification (Australian Sports Commission, 1996). The game design method of deliberately modifying by adapting and constraining games to condition game forms and create play with purpose is the process of 'eliminating, refining, simplifying or adding to game rules and playing conditions to focus attention on specific technical or tactical game understanding' through a game form (Pill, 2013, p. 9). In the Australian sport landscape, one of the first coaches to write about coaching this way was Eric Worthington (1974), and the combining of technical and tactical learning through game form is evident in Rick Charlesworth's explanation of 'designer games' (Charlesworth, 1994).

The Spectrum of Teaching Styles

Having explained the GSA as play with purpose, we now turn our attention to explaining why it should be viewed as a cluster of teaching styles and not just 'guided discovery'. We do this by using the Spectrum of Teaching Styles (the Spectrum) as a lens on the GSA. The Spectrum is a theory constructed from the premise that 'teaching' is directed by a single unifying process, decision-making. Specifically, who is making the decisions, when the decisions are being made, and the intent of these decisions (Mosston & Ashworth, 2008).

The Spectrum (Mosston & Ashworth, 2008) constitutes 11 teaching styles, on a continuum from most teacher controlled to least teacher controlled (Figure 1.2). In Command Style, the teacher (coach) is making the maximum amount of decisions and the learner (player) the minimum. When a Self Teaching Style is used, the teacher is making the minimum amount of decisions and the learner is making the maximum. Put in another way, there is less coach direction at the Self Teaching Style than there is at the Command Style (Figure 1.2).

The first five teaching styles of Command Style through to Inclusion Style are known as *reproduction* cluster teaching styles as they require the use of existing (known, past) information and knowledge by the players. Essentially the player is asked to reproduce known knowledge or skills that the coach will have demonstrated or asked them to reproduce. The remaining styles, Guided Discovery through to the Self-Teaching Style, form a cluster that invites the *production* (discovery) of new knowledge by the player/s (Mosston & Ashworth, 2008).

Responsibility for decision making

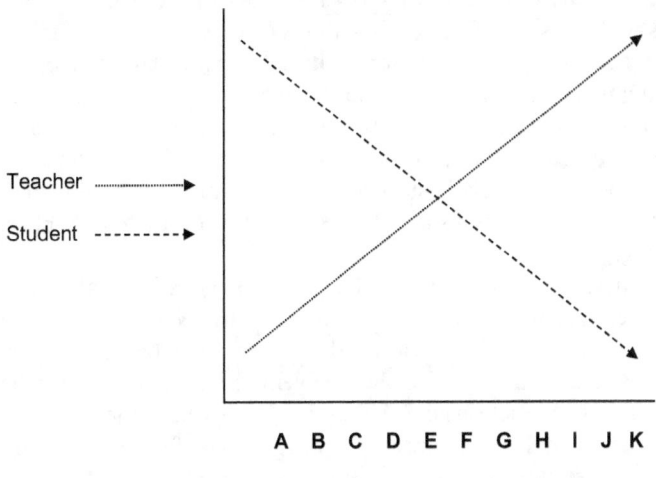

Figure 1.2 Mosston and Ashworth's Spectrum of Teaching Styles and the degree of teacher (coach) and student (player) decision making.
Source: Mosston & Ashworth (2008)

The Game Sense approach: deliberate design through The Spectrum lens

The Spectrum provides a lens through which to view the instruction decision-making made in the GSA model (Figure 1.1). In a GSA, it was originally suggested that game play commence after a warm-up (Australian Sports Commission, 1996). In our experience, a warm-up often looks like a progress from closed to open drills: meaning the movements become less predictable or have more variables for the athlete to process as the warm-up progresses. For example, in a throwing sport this may be as simple as throwing and catching with a partner over 10 metres. This is assumed to be Practice Style as the athletes are reproducing a known movement and focusing on accuracy and 'warming-up' muscles. The coach may (or may not circulate) and provide feedback to the athletes regarding technique or accuracy. This has the hallmarks of Practice Style as it involves 'practice of a memory/reproduction task with private feedback' (Mosston & Ashworth, 2008, p. 94). As the players warm-up, the distance may increase requiring judgment of distance, trajectory and force, however the teaching style being used would still represent Practice Style as the athlete would be referring to past experiences as to how to throw accurately. The coach could manipulate task constraints and reduce the time to identify flight or trajectory of the ball (e.g. Partner 1 begins with eyes closed. Partner 2 throws the ball in the air and shouts 'now' when the ball is at the top of its flight path. Partner 1 opens eyes and attempts to catch ball). While this has made the skill more difficult to perform (as it has reduced the time to process and react) it is still Practice Style as the athlete is recalling known movement patterns to achieve the task. If this basic structure of a warm-up, progressing from closed to more open skills is followed then it is most likely Practice Style coaching.

Considering Game 1 (Figure 1.1), if the players knew the answer to the tactical problem or concept in focus set by the coach then it would be most likely Practice Style as the players will be recalling known solutions and skills to solve the problem. In a situation such as this, Game 1 has characteristics of Practice Style where the coach 'moves from learner to learner, observing both the performance of the task and the decision making process, then offers feedback and moves on to the next learner' (Mosston & Ashworth, 2008, p. 95). However, if in Game 1 the solution is unknown to the player/s, then it has characteristics of either Convergent Discovery or Divergent Discovery Styles, depending on how many solutions the coach seeks the player to produce. For example, Divergent Discovery style is characterised by the player being required to 'discover divergent (multiple) responses to a single question/situation, within a specific cognitive operation' (Mosston & Ashworth, 2008, p. 247). Convergent Discovery style differs in that it requires one solution to a problem to be produced. Both these styles are from the *production* cluster of the Spectrum, as players must be producing knowledge new to themselves – not recalling known information.

At the point of reflection in Figure 1.1, the coach may have identified that some players do not have the skills to satisfy the challenge of play and therefore cannot satisfactorily solve the tactical problem. At this point, the coach may decide that deliberate practice is necessary in a more closed environment than Game 1 provided. If this is the case, the coach will most likely choose Practice Style coaching. Another option that the coach could choose is from the *reproduction* cluster, known as Inclusion Style. This style is characterised by the coach selecting subject matter tasks and designing multiple levels of difficulty for each task. The players select the level of difficulty that is appropriate to their performance. During the activity, the players check their performance using a coach prepared set of criteria. The coach circulates among the practice activities to ask questions for clarification to affirm the accuracy of the players' assessment of their performance or to redirect the player's focus to specific performance details on the criteria. Performance standards need to be met before players can move from one level of difficulty to another or return to Game 1.

After the player/s have practiced the skill to a level that would allow them to participate more effectively in Game 1 (whether that be through Inclusion Style or Practice Style) the coach may return players to Game 1 setting the same tactical problem to be solved. Again, this would be either Convergent Discovery Style or Divergent Discovery Style instruction depending on the amount of solutions to be discovered or created. The other option presented in Figure 1.1 is that some players may be making the same mistakes over and over (reflecting that they may not be aware of the tactical concept or principle of play). The coach may scaffold open-ended questions to the player/s to lead them to discover the principle or tactic. This is a deliberate pedagogy of scaffolding questions to lead to the discovery of a principle. The instruction style is Guided Discovery Style. The Spectrum defines the Guided Discovery Style as 'the logical and sequential design of questions that lead a person to discover a predetermined response' (Mosston & Ashworth, 2008, p. 212). Once the concept or principal is discovered, the coach may cycle back to Game 1 to allow the players to now practice applying the principal or tactic in the game environment to consolidate the learning (Figure 1.1). However, the tactical principle is understood, and the player/s will attempt to recall the understanding to solve the tactical problem. This game has the hallmarks of a Practice Style due to the tactic being recalled and not discovered.

After this process has occurred (i.e. the player/s have discovered the tactic or principle/s and are now playing the game recalling known tactics and strategies and known skills at the appropriate time) the coach may decide to move on to Game 2 to progress the learning. At this point that the coach will again set a tactical problem to be solved (meaning *production* cluster styles will deliberately be used by the coach) and the process described earlier will occur again based on the factors the coach observes and the needs of the players as learners.

The final stage of the model is the warm down, which includes functional training or tactical practice. This has been defined earlier as either set plays or phase practice (understanding between small groups of players). Like the examples given above, set plays can be directly taught with no defenders so the attackers initially learn a simple pattern. The athletes may walk through the movements, learning timing and cues and perhaps even initially told to run to markers. In this case, we argue that this is Practice Style as a model of movement would be demonstrated/shown and the athletes would be asked to reproduce the movement and pattern. The coach may choose to increase the complexity of this set play by including defenders (may be passive or active) and the players will run the set play at real speed. The defenders are in place for opposition. In some situations, this could be as simple as an 'if–then–because' response. As a simple example of 'if–then–because' production thinking, if the defender goes left then you go right because the space is available. In these cases, we suggest that this is Practice Style. We do not argue that the complexity of the decision is not getting progressively more difficult, all that is being suggested is that in this example, the players attacking know what to do. The coach has not suggested that they need to search or discover an answer. If the players do not know the answer, then the episode could demonstrate characteristics of a Convergent Discovery episode where the athlete is being asked to discover an 'if–then–because' solution – one solution to a problem.

Conclusion

In this chapter we have shown the GSA model as play with purpose (Figure 1.1) to clearly demonstrate a GSA as a toolkit of teaching styles (SueSee et al., 2016; SueSee & Pill, 2018). This idea is not new with some (SueSee et al., 2016) suggesting that a GSA is often not one style but a cluster of styles. Being a cluster of styles neither rejects nor accepts only one teaching style but embraces styles for the aims they can achieve (Mosston & Ashworth, 2008). It is therefore a 'non-versus' approach to pedagogy. Teaching styles like Convergent Discovery and Divergent Discovery can create learning episodes that require the player to use resourcefulness to solve problems, thus developing thinking players who can 'creatively' solve problems (SueSee & Pill, 2018).

This chapter has outlined the styles that may come into use during a GSA coaching session by using The Spectrum (Mosston & Ashworth, 2008) to highlight the decisions being made during the learning episodes. We have shown that a GSA can be considered a cluster of teaching styles used to achieve a variety of aims as no one style can address the complex and unique needs (physical, cognitive etc.) of players in a practice session.

References

Australian Sports Commission. (1996). *Game sense: perceptions and actions: Research report*. Belconnen, ACT: Australian Sports Commission.

Breed, R. & Spittle, M. (2011). *Developing game sense through tactical learning: A resource for teachers and coaches*. Melbourne, Vic: Cambridge University Press.
Charlesworth, R. (1994). Designer games. *Sport Coach*, 17(4), 30–33.
den Duyn, N. (1997a) Game sense: It's time to play. *Sports Coach*, 19(4), 9–11.
den Duyn, N. (1997b). *Game sense: Developing thinking players workbook*. Canberra, ACT: Australian Sports Commission.
Fischer, A., Reilly, J., Kelly, L., Montgomery, C., Williamson, A., Paton, J. & Grant, S. (2005). Fundamental movement skills and habitual physical activity in young children. *Medicine and Science in Sports and Exercise*, 37(4), 684–688.
Hattie, J. & Yates, S. (2014). Understanding learning: Lessons for learning, teaching and research. Retrieved from http://research.acer.edu.au/cgi/view content.cgi?article=1207&context=research_conference.
Hendry, D. T. & Hodges, N. J. (2019). Pathways to expert performance in soccer. *Journal of Expertise*, 2(1), 1–13.
Kirk, D. (2010). *Physical education futures*. London: Routledge.
Light, R. (2004). Coaches' experiences of game sense: Opportunities and challenges. *Physical Education and Sport Pedagogy*, 9(2), 115–131.
Light, R. (2006). Game sense: Innovation or just good coaching? *Journal of Physical Education New Zealand*, 39(1), 8–19.
Light, R. (2013). *Game sense: Pedagogy for performance, participation and enjoyment*. New York: Routledge.
Memmert, D. (2015). *Teaching tactical creativity in sport*. New York: Routledge.
Mosston, M. & Ashworth, S. (2008). Teaching physical education. San Francisco, CA: Benjamin Cummings. Retrieved from www.spectrumofteaching styles.org/e-book-download.php.
Pill, S. (2007). *Play with Purpose: A resource to support teachers in the implementation of the game-centred approach to physical education*. Adelaide, SA: ACHPER Publications.
Pill, S. (2012). Teaching game sense in soccer. *Journal of Physical Education, Recreation and Dance*, 83(3), 42–52.
Pill, S. (2013). *Play with purpose: Game sense to sport literacy*. Hindmarsh, SA: ACHPER Publications.
Pill, S. (2014). Informing Game Sense pedagogy with constraints led theory for coaching in Australian football. *Sport Coaching Review*, 3(1), 46–62.
Pill, S. (2015). Implementing game sense coaching approach in Australian football through action research. *Agora for Physical Education and Sport*, 18(1), 1–19.
Pill, S. (2016). Game sense: Developing thinking players. In M. Drummond & S. Pill (eds), *Advances in Australian football: A sociological and applied science exploration of the game* (pp. 42–49). Hindmarsh, SA: ACHPER Publications.
Pill, S. (2017). The game sense approach as explicit teaching and deliberate practice. In J.Williams & R. Dodd (eds), *Edited proceedings of the 30th*

ACHPER International Conference, 16–18 January (pp. 133–144). Hindmarsh, SA: ACHPER Publications.

Rankin, J., Pill, S. & Magias, T. (2018). Informing the coaching pedagogy of game modification in a game sense approach with affordance theory. *Ágora para la Educación Física y el Deporte*, 20(1), 68–89.

Schembri, G. (2005). *Playing for life: Coach's guide*. Canberra, ACT: Australian Sports Commission.

Sport Australia. (2019). Playing for life resources. Retrieved from www.sportingschools.gov.au/resources-and-pd/schools/playing-for-life-resources.

Sport Australia. (2020). Playing for life. Retrieved from www.sportaus.gov.au/p4l.

SueSee, B., Pill, S. & Edwards, K. (2016). Reconciling approaches – a game centred approach to sport teaching and Mosston's spectrum of teaching styles. *European Journal of Physical Education and Sport Science*, 2(4), 69–86.

SueSee, B., & Pill, S. (2018) Game-based teaching and coaching as a toolkit of teaching styles. *Strategies: A Journal for Physical and Sport Educators*, 31(5), 21–28.

Worthington, E. (1974). *Learning and teaching soccer skills*. North Hollywood, CA: Hal Leighton.

2 Digital video games as a game-based coaching tool

Amy Price

Game-based coaching: different tools do different things

The offering of game-based coaching approaches is wide ranging and discerning between each approach is probably the most challenging task facing coaches who aim to be intentional with their coaching practice. It is not possible for any coaching approach to 'do everything' for player development, and therefore the first step for a coach when deciding what approach to use and when to use it, is to establish how it is likely to positively impact player learning and performance. The analogy of game-based approaches as tools in a coach's tool kit demonstrates the theoretical and conceptual nuances between a set of tools and highlights the need for different tools to be explicit about the impact they claim to have.

The purpose of this chapter is to introduce a different tool to the coach's game based tool box, known as a Digital Video Games Approach (DVGA) (Price, Collins, Stoszkowski & Pill, 2017) which is inspired by digital video game design, and the notion of sport coaches and video game designers having similar goals (Pill, 2014). In introducing this game-based coaching tool, this chapter will explicitly highlight the role of metacognition as a theoretical underpinning for a DVGA and its proposed impact on players' strategic understanding of how to play games. The pedagogical principles of a DVGA will be used as a framework to provide examples of its application in two contrasting team games. Lastly, this chapter will offer insights from a sample of youth soccer coaches concerning their interpretation of strategic understanding and the methods deployed for developing this element of game understanding.

Good Digital Game Design

According to Gee (2003), digital games are long, hard and challenging yet still enjoyable to do. A possible explanation for this statement is that all good digital games are designed using similar principles, and these principles provide high potential for both learning and performance: empowered learners; problem solving; deep understanding. Gee (2013) refers to a framework for Good Digital Game Design, consisting of 13 design features which are used for designing games or game like experiences (e.g. 'well-ordered problems') (for a detailed list of design features, see Gee, 2013, p. 23–36). Where a game is stronger on any of these features, the better the game is for learning (Gee, 2013). This chapter will focus on how these 13 design features impact the principle of 'deep understanding' for sport and games. Deep understanding is considered a significant principle for various game-based coaching tools because of their consistent emphasis on developing tactical understanding and tactical awareness and appreciation (Stolz & Pill, 2014; Kinnerk, Harvey, MacDonncha & Lyons, 2018).

Strategic understanding for games

When coaching team or individual sport using a game-based approach, designing practice that supports player understanding of the game's internal logic (Grehaigne & Godbout, 1997), or to appreciate the game's tactical principles of play (Wade, 1967) should be prioritised. Understanding the game's logic or tactical principles is usually guided by an intention of 'outwitting' or gaining an advantage over your opponent in order to progress in the game (Almond, 1986). In doing so, the player needs to draw upon their declarative knowledge *about* the game (e.g. about a particular tactic, about passing, about the game's rules), and their procedural knowledge of *how* to execute actions in the game (e.g. how to use a particular tactic, how to pass, how to manipulate the game's rules). In demonstrating a *deep* understanding of the game, the player will realise when and why to engage with declarative and procedural knowledge bases in order to consciously seek to outwit their opponent. This is known as using conditional knowledge bases, or otherwise described as thinking strategically or having a strategic understanding of the game (Price, Collins, Stoszkowski & Pill, 2020).

For games players, thinking strategically is particularly important due to the dynamic and complex nature of games themselves. Events that occur in any one game can never occur in the same way again (Storey & Butler, 2012) and so requires game players to be responsive to: the task at hand (in order to be successful considering factors such as score line, time remaining, weather conditions, substitutions); the opposition (their capabilities, common play configurations dictated by them); self and team mates (mine and our capabilities, our goals for play configurations); personal learning strategies (remaining motivated, removing obstacles for learning). As a result of the game's complexity, players with a deep understanding of the game will continuously (during game play) plan for, monitor, and evaluate their approach towards outwitting the opponent, using the many variable events that will occur in a game. Indeed, players who use conditional knowledge bases in game play are flexible in their approach to deciding on an optimum action for a given moment in the game, and capable of rationalising their choice in relation to what they know about how they are thinking.

Metacognition for games players

When thinking about one's own thinking during game play, different types of games afford different quantities and segments of time. For example, basketball (invasion) is fast paced with a relatively small number of players on court, compared with cricket (striking and fielding) where there are sometimes greater amounts of time in between significant events. However, despite there being strong or weak time constraints, Price, Collins, Stoszkowski and Pill (2019) argued that time should not be a factor which can dictate the extent to which a player thinks on a meta-level. Dating back to the work of Flavell (1979), metacognition was introduced as a theory to understand the self-regulation of cognitive activities during a situation where learning is possible. In the context of playing a game, there is almost always opportunity for players to engage in a learning process, since as I have already explained, the problems presented in any one game are never the same.

Cognition and metacognition overlap, and so, I refer to Flavell's (1979) distinction where cognition is to think about how to solve a problem in order to make progress, and metacognition is to think about how one is thinking about how to solve a problem to monitor progress. The purpose of metacognition for games players is not to enhance visual perception, attention, decision making, or problem solving because these are all perceptual-cognitive skills common to game-based approaches. Thus, the purpose of metacognition for games players is to become aware of how to regulate and control one's own thought processes as they play the game.

Metacognitive game skills

Thinking on a meta-level requires players to consciously control how they use information concerning the task at hand, the game itself, people playing the game, and personal learning strategies to plan how an advantage is gained, and how this advantage can be self-monitored and evaluated – during the game itself. Controlling one's own thinking by deliberately accessing these sources of information at the appropriate time and with the appropriate frequency is a non-linear process and requires ongoing adjustments of planning, monitoring and evaluating. In the context of games, Price and colleagues referred to three 'metacognitive game skills' (Price et al., 2019, p. 129–130) as a framework for distinguishing how and why a player would attempt to control their own thinking as they play the game (see Table 2.1). These are: deliberate thinking and action; meta-level problem solving; good learners and teachers.

Importantly for sport coaching practitioners, metacognitive game skills are transferable between game contexts and game categories (Price et al., 2019). Therefore, the value in developing metacognitive game skills might be more, as we have stressed that no one game is ever the same, and knowing that competition contexts is inevitable (against an unknown opposition and without opportunity for much guidance from the coach) (Price et al., manuscript in preparation).

Digital Video Games Approach (DVGA) for coaching games

To develop players metacognitive game skills, Price et al. (2017) suggested a game-based coaching approach – DVGA, that is characterised by five pedagogical principles (see Table 2.2). The five principles stem from Gee's (2003, 2007, 2013) conceptual work on Good Game Design, and Flavell's (1979) theory of metacognition. DVGA adopts the premise originally stated by Gee (2013), that where a game is stronger on any of these pedagogical principles, the better it is for learning.

To justify why and when a coach would choose to use this game-based coaching approach, we emphasise the proposed impact on player learning and performance is metacognitive game skills, or to develop a 'deep understanding' of how to play games. While, unintentional benefits are likely to include player engagement, enjoyment and motivation, because we should not separate good learning from enjoyment or enjoyment from good learning (Gee, 2003).

When designing game-based practice using DVGA, it is imperative that the internal logic (Grehaigne & Godbout, 1997) remains intact. Similar to other game-based approaches, without the representation of problems which occur in the actual game, practice becomes decontextualised and lacking meaning. In digital video games and Gee's

Table 2.1 Metacognitive game skills with examples from game two contrasting game categories.

Metacognitive game skill	Examples
Deliberate Thinking and Action (planning and re-planning strategy)	**Invasion:** planning to change the way we attack in wide areas on the right side of the pitch by creating 2v1 opportunities, because we realise our wide right players are especially effective at interchanging positions, against defenders who are poor at tracking and marking.
	Striking & Fielding: planning how to reach the target score, set by the opposition. We decide to target the opening bowlers while they are only allowed two fielders to protect the boundary and the ball is in its newest conditions. Therefore, we can target the boundaries while the ball is hard.
Meta-level Problem Solving (replying to a problem by setting the opponent a problem)	**Invasion:** inviting the opposition goal keeper, who is effective at passing and supporting, to play out to a defender who we have established is less comfortable in possession, and then pressing the defender so that possession is lost near the opponent's goal area.
	Striking & Fielding: the opposition have scored heavily against our quicker bowlers, but we know they will struggle to maintain that scoring with pace off the ball. Therefore, we introduce spin from both ends meaning they will not be able to use pace off the ball and will need to find a new method to score.
Good Learners and Teachers (players identify what they need to find out, and set out to find it)	**Invasion:** upon loosing possession, remaining high in wide areas to test if the opposition's wide players will stay to defend the counter or join in with their attack.
	Striking & Fielding: opening batters use the early deliveries bowled to them to determine the pace and bounce off the pitch. Opening batters communicate their observations to the rest of the team via the substitutes or once they are dismissed. Information can be used to determine how to bat and bowl on the pitch, and to predict target scores.

Source: adapted from Price, Collins, Stoszkowski & Pill (in preparation)

features for Good Digital Game Design, this is known as 'situated meanings' or 'meaning as action and image' (Gee, 2007, 2013). Situated meanings is when a person associates images, action or goals with experiences. In the context of a game-based approach, players are more likely to relate to the game's demands (such as problems) if they are experiencing these problems for themselves. From a metacognitive view

Table 2.2 Pedagogical principles for a Digital Video Games Approach.

Principle	Characteristics	Impact on metacognitive game skills
What's the Mission?	• No technical/skill/tactical focus • Emphasis on players' strategising and re-strategising • Coach mindset shifts from 'this is what we will we be learning today' to 'this is today's mission'	• Being flexible with plan of what, when, how and why to play the game • Responding to the game and opponent, not just satisfying a coaching curriculum
Using the Pause Button	• Integrating varying degrees of support for players via the '4 C's' – Cheat, Change, Clue, Challenge • Players decide when, how and with what they'd like support via the '4 C's' • Coach mindset shifts from 'how can I help or challenge the players' to 'how are players responding to the mission'	• Slowing down the game so that players develop their ability to think on a meta-level • Encouraging players to self-direct their own learning against what is actually happening in the game
Level-Up!	• Complexity (variations of time and space) moves from simple to complex levels, where players can be on different levels within the same game • Initial assessment of players occurs via their metacognitive skills • Coach mindset shifts from 'what's my next progression for this practice' to 'who's likely to level-up next'?	• Highlighting to players/teams the need to monitor where they are at in reaching the game's mission • Emphasising the need to concentrate on the opposition • Providing feedback to players/teams on when/how they've been successful
Earning a Super Power	• Providing players with the opportunity to be more effective for a short period of time • Players decide when and why they need the power, and how best to use it • Coach mindset shifts from 'how do I adjust the task to meet the ability of all players' to 'what super power might be helpful for players to earn'	• Giving players an option to self-evaluate their own capabilities and impact on the game • Offering players the chance to experience the game with a new or different skill set, in order to establish what is needed to progress in the game

(continued)

Table 2.2 (continued)

Principle	Characteristics	Impact on metacognitive game skills
Saving Progress	• Individual players/teams end and re-start the game at different points and therefore with a challenge point that is relevant • Players are inclined to take risks in game play because the game won't allow for regression • Coach mindset shifts from 'we need to cover all of this technical or tactical content' to 'let's allow the players to spend time mastering this game'	• Encouraging players/teams to rethink how they're currently thinking about how to play the game • Ensuring that both teams experience the need to confront situations which are not easy

Source: adapted from Price et al. (2019, p. 129)

point, experiencing first hand and authentic problems by nature means that there will be an opponent involved in the practice, and the practice will demand certain intentions and actions distinct to the game category (e.g. invasion games requires teams to defend one area and attack another). Consequently, there is a greater possibility for players to consciously intend on outwitting the opponent by thinking about how one is thinking about how to respond to the opponent to monitor progress in the game.

Strategic understanding: thoughts from professional youth soccer coaches in England

Professional youth (boys) soccer teams in England have extensive training programs where opportunity for coaches to coach the players in practice and competition is between 6–8 hours per week (Premier League, 2011). Price et al. (2020) conducted interviews with a range of professional youth coaches at seven Premier League Academies in England, who coach players from between the ages of 9 and 23. The purpose of these interviews was to establish how the coaches interpreted the term 'strategic understanding', in addition to gaining insight on the methods deployed by the coaches to improve this element of game understanding (cf. Price et al. 2020 for in depth information for methods and methodology).

The findings of this study demonstrated four higher order themes (each with two lower order themes) which represented potential challenges with developing players strategic understanding of the game:

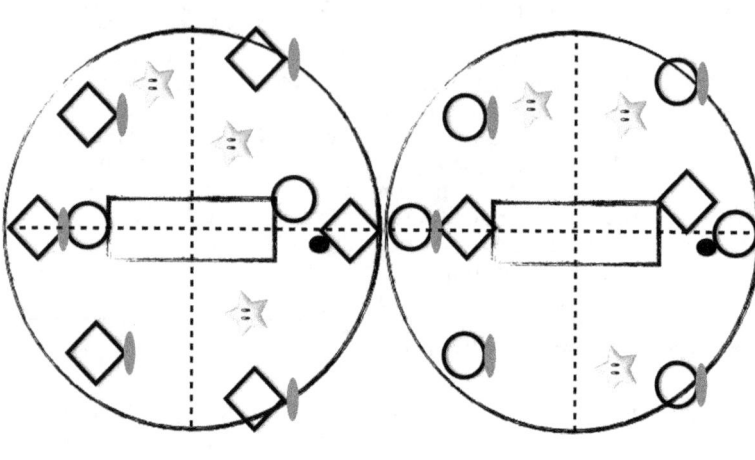

Mission: to unlock your fielders from their red spot

Level Up: by conceding lowest number of runs in 2 overs
Tutorial friendly
Level 1 1 fielder unlocked
Level 2 2 fielder unlocked
Level 3 3 fielder unlocked
Level 4 4 fielder unlocked
Level 5 everyone unlocked
Boss Level
*fielder can move from red spot as soon as bowler releases ball

Super Power: earn power by running over token with individual possession of ball (when ball is in play)

Mario Star
Available for the fielding team only:
- 2 runs to opposition's score

Game Pauses: decided by the (fielding) player or team

Cheat	maximum support	*skip a level*
Change	work together	*modify playing area*
Clue	prompt	*think about areas of the field where you gain the greatest advantage*
Challenge	make the task more difficult	*play in three quarter's of the area*

Figure 2.1 Using a Digital Video Games approach for cricket.

Mission: to stay in the final!

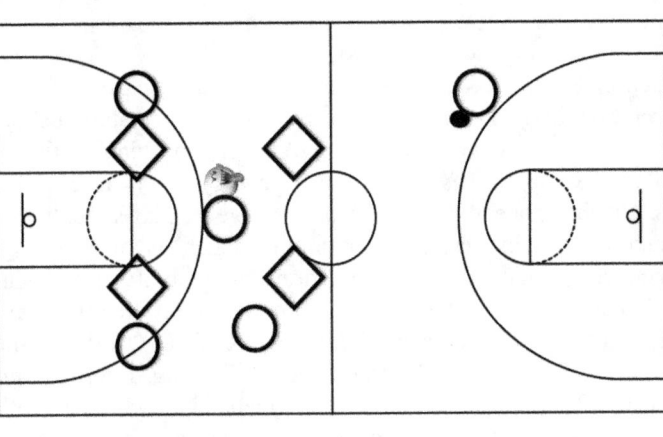

Level Up: by winning a game
Tutorial friendly
Level 1 group stage (basket worth 5)
Level 2 last 16 (basket worth 4)
Level 3 3 quarter final (basket worth 3)
Level 4 2 semi final (basket worth 2)
Level 5 final (basket worth 1)
Boss Level

Super Power: earn power by holding token when your team have possession of the ball

Mario Ghost
use the ball freely in both keys (no steals or interceptions)

Game Pauses: decided by the player or team

Cheat	maximum support	*disallow an opponent's basket*
Change	work together	*modify opponent's set up*
Clue	prompt	*think about areas of the court where you are most vulnerable*
Challenge	make the task more difficult	*play on 4 professional fouls*

Figure 2.2 Using a Digital Video Games approach for basketball.

maintaining control of game play (playing in a style that represents identity of the soccer club & following game plans), players as problem solvers (game management, dealing with change), player reflection (reflecting on and in performance, having a why behind game actions), individuals within a team (playing to strengths, recognising opportunities to practice individual targets).

In summary, the coaches interviewed did not share a consistent interpretation of a player who has a strategic understanding of the game, and nor did coaches apply any specific coaching method that sought to develop this aspect of their players' understanding. Nonetheless, coaches appeared to agree on a range of player qualities that demonstrate superior game understanding (such as reflection, game management, justification of game actions, adaptability and playing to strengths), and some of these qualities are also supported in other studies that investigated metacognition for sport (Dail, 2014; MacIntrye, Igou, Campbell, Moran & Matthews, 2014; Toering, Elferink-Gemser & Visscher, 2009). The coaches viewed metacognitive game skills as valued aspects of player performance, so long as coaches continued to have some degree of control over not just what the players do on the field, but also what they are thinking about how they are thinking on the field.

The findings of this study yield interest for practitioners in both professional and recreational sport because competition contexts dictate situations where players are required to monitor how and when their future performance is to be enhanced, independently from the coach. The competition context (the game itself) is a complex and dynamic environment where no coach ever 'gets it right' all of the time when judging when to interfere with play for a coaching intervention, how to pre-empt players with instruction or guidance, or why to generate reflective questioning in breaks of play and after play. Therefore, when players can regulate and control their own thinking during game play, it is logical to believe players themselves are also acting as their own personal coach.

Summary

In this chapter, I have highlighted the significance of coaches to make conscious and informed decisions for the benefit of player learning regarding which game-based coaching tool to use, when to use it, and why to use it. This is because different tools have been designed to achieve different outcomes for player development. If the coach sees value in helping players to think and act strategically during game play, then I argue that a DVGA for coaching games is a suitable game-based coaching tool. A DVGA exposes players to practice that seeks to hone their metacognitive game skills, so that players will become better at learning how to understand how to play the game. For players of any age and stage of development, the ability to control how one is thinking about how to outwit the opponent is an important quality so that players can monitor their own progress in game play. As such, coaches who include this game-based coaching approach within their curriculum, in addition to alternative game-based approaches (such as TGfU, Game Sense, and others) will be offering both metacognitive and cognitive opportunities for player development.

References

Almond, L. (1986). Games making. In R. Thorpe, D. Bunker & L. Almond (eds), *Rethinking Games Teaching* (pp. 35–44). Loughborough: University of Technology Loughborough.
Dail, T. K. (2014). Metacognition and coaching: How to develop a thinking athlete. *Journal of Physical Education, Recreation & Dance, 85*(5), 49–51.
Flavell, J. H. (1979). Metacognition and cognitive monitoring. *American Psychologist, 34*(10), 906–911.
Gee, J. P. (2003). *What video games have to teach us about learning and literacy.* New York: Palgrave Macmillan.
Gee, J. P. (2007). *Good video games and good learning: New literacies and digital epistemologies.* New York: Peter Lang Publishing.
Gee, J. P. (2013). *Good video games and learning.* New York: Peter Lang Publishing.
Grehaigne, J. F. & Godbout, P. (1997). The teaching of tactical knowledge in team sports. *Journal of Canadian Association of Physical Education, Recreation and Dance, 61*, 46–51.
Kinnerk, P., Harvey, S., MacDonncha, C. & Lyons, M. (2018). A review of the game-based approaches to coaching literature in competitive team sport settings. *Quest, 70*(4), 401–418.
MacIntrye, T.E., Igou, E.R., Campbell, M.J., Moran, A.P. & Matthews, J. (2014). Metacognition and action: a new pathway to understanding social and cognitive aspects of expertise in sport. *Frontiers in Psychology, 5*, 1155.
Pill, S. (2014). What does it mean for pedagogy to think like a game developer? *Journal of Physical Education, Recreation and Dance, 85(1)*, 9–15.
Premier League (2011). Elite player performance plan (EPPP). Retrieved from www.goalreports.com/EPLPlan.pdf.
Price, A., Collins, D., Stoszkowski, J. & Pill, S. (2017). Learning to play soccer: Lessons on meta-cognition from video game design. *Quest, 70*(3), 321–333.
Price, A., Collins, D., Stoszkowski, J. & Pill, S. (2019). Coaching games: Comparisons and contrasts. *International Sport Coaching Journal, 6*(1), 126–131.

Price, A., Collins, D., Stoszkowski, J. & Pill, S. (2020). Strategic understandings: An investigation of professional academy youth soccer coaches' interpretation, knowledge and application of metacognition. *International Sport Coaching Journal*, 7(2), 151–162.

Price, A., Collins, D., Stoszkowski, J. & Pill, S. (in preparation). Operationalising and testing the validity of a multi-method approach to measuring understanding in the development of games players.

Stolz, S. & Pill, S. (2014). Teaching games and sport for understanding: Exploring and reconsidering its relevance in physical education. *European Physical Education Review*, 20(1), 36–71.

Storey, B. & Butler, J. (2012). Complexity thinking in PE: game-centred approaches, games as complex adaptive systems, and ecological values, *Physical Education and Sport Pedagogy*, 18(2), 133–149.

Toering, T. T., Elferink-Gemser, M. T., Jordet, G. & Visscher, C. (2009). Self-regulation and performance level of elite and non-elite youth soccer players. *Journal of Sports Sciences*, 27, 1509–1517.

Wade, A. (1967). *The FA guide to training and coaching*. London: Heinemann.

3 Developing Thinking Players

Barrie Gordon

The genesis for the Developing Thinking Players (DTP^{TM}) game-based pedagogy (Gordon, 2015) is the Teaching Games for Understanding (TGfU) model (Bunker & Thorpe, 1982). DTP^{TM} is also aligned with the core tenets of game-based philosophy. Where DTP^{TM} differs from many game-based approaches is in its strong emphasis on developing tactical understanding and good decision-making during the initial stages of learning the game. These two areas are the framework from which a mature sense of the game is developed (Gordon, 2015). Developing tactical understanding and decision-making with players who may have limited skills and/or knowledge of the game is achieved in the DTP^{TM} approach through extensive use of modified equipment and rules. This chapter will describe the DTP^{TM} approach and use coaching baseball/softball as a context to illustrate DTP^{TM} in practice. While baseball/softball is used in this instance, the principles of DTP^{TM} are applicable to most other games and sports.

Tactical understanding

A tenet of the DTP^{TM} approach is that with modifications to equipment and rules players can develop sophisticated tactical understanding, independent of their levels of skill and experience. For this reason, the DTP^{TM} approach keeps tactical understanding at the forefront of coaching sessions, as this can be the foundation from which all other learning occurs. Tactical understanding is also an area of games and sports that many participants find both challenging and engaging, and gaining tactical appreciation adds an element of enjoyment to the experience.

Decision-making

Strongly associated with developing an understanding of tactics, is the need for players to become good decision makers so they can successfully act on that understanding. To become good decision makers, players need to have opportunities to practice making decisions in authentic practical contexts. This should include having the opportunity to experience the outcomes of their decision-making, either positive or negative, and to reflect on what, if anything, they would do differently if they found themselves in a similar situation in the future (Araújo, Hristovski, Seifert, Carvalho & Davids, 2019).

Modified equipment and rules

One criticism of games and athlete centred approaches is that learning tactics will be limited because 'an initial level of control of a ball is necessary before tactics can be employed in most elementary game settings' (Turner, 2018, p. 130). The DTP^{TM} approach addresses this through extensive use of modified equipment and rule changes. This allows players to concentrate on developing a level of tactical understanding and decision-making. A player learning baseball or softball, for example, needs to be able to consider 'what is' the best decision tactically when deciding which base to throw the ball to. The opportunity to carefully consider the options will be lost if concerns around a lack of proficiency in using a glove to field a hard-hit ball distracts, and possibly overwhelms, a player. It is for this reason that in coaching the baseball or softball activities presented below, there will be differences from the normal game in the equipment used, and in the way that the activities and games are played. In the initial stage, with inexperienced players, soft easily caught balls are used and for many of the activities the 'batter' throws the ball, with a single bounce, directly to a fielder and no gloves are used. At all times the intention is to establish a practical context that allows players to consider, and then enact tactical decisions.

A decision on the degree to which equipment will be modified is dependent on the level of proficiency that the players have. In a situation where you are working with skilled players, who are fully capable of concentrating on their decision-making, there may well be no need to modify equipment.

Skill development

The DTP approach is a holistic approach underpinned by the understanding that learning appropriate physical skills is an important part of developing quality players. It is based on a belief that the motivation to learn physical skills is enhanced when players have a clear understanding of why the skills are important within the game context. A player who knows that they need to successfully field the ball, pivot and throw accurately to second base to get the lead runner, but fails to achieve this in an authentic context, will then be motivated to learn how to do so. This motivation will be higher than if the skills were taught in isolation with no game related context to place them in (Konings & Hettinga, 2018).

Questioning and discussion

A central requirement of the DTP^{TM} approach is the need for the coach to question players and hold discussions in ways that supports the learning process. It is important that the players are engaged fully as participants as this engagement helps them achieve a deeper level of understanding than often occurs in the more traditional coach-directed sessions (Harvey, Cope & Jones, 2016; Harvey & Light, 2015). It is also important in these discussions that there is a balance between considering what went well and what didn't.

It is often easier to concentrate on problems that you have identified than it is to acknowledge the positive. In many cases, when a positive outcome occurs, players will be unsure why and how it happened. It is important, therefore, that you consciously take any opportunity to address success when it happens. By doing so you offer positive reinforcement to the players and help them generate a deeper awareness which will increase the chances of the positive play reoccurring. This does not mean that weaknesses in the player's tactical awareness and mistakes that they have made should not also be openly addressed.

'Good questions need to take the learner beyond the recall of basic information and challenge. Meaningful questions breed more questions and the desire to find answers' (Pate, 2012, p. 28). An example is a coach asking a player; 'Was throwing to first base the right decision?' Asking instead; 'What were the reasons that made you decide to throw to first base rather than to second?' requires a deeper level of cognitive engagement from the player.

Examples of questions that coaches could ask include:

1 In the last play, we achieved two outs which is a great outcome. What did you do to make it happen? How do you think we could increase the chances of it happening again?
2 Explain why you ... What would you do next time?

3   In that last play, the opposition scored two runs and you got no outs. What do you think happened? If that situation happens again, what are you going to do?
4   As a team what do think should happen when ...?
5   Batting team, you chose to throw to the shortstop with runners on first and second base. What was the thinking behind that decision? What were the risks and rewards involved? Would you do the same the next time? Why or why not?

Developing thinking players in baseball/softball

The following activities and games are designed to illustrate the DTP^{TM} approach to coaching using the context of baseball/softball. While there are obvious differences between the two games, there are also numerous commonalities both tactically and in the specific decision-making that is required to play the game(s) well. The activities and games are designed to give players an opportunity to gain a tactical understanding of the game, to practice their decision-making and to enact this decision-making in practice.

The activities that follow use equipment (e.g. soft balls) and rules (e.g. throwing ball not hitting it) that are appropriate for players with little experience through to those with medium levels of knowledge. You can modify these to accommodate more skilled and knowledgeable players as long as the skill requirements don't influence their ability to fully engage with tactics and decision-making.

Activity one

This is an introductory warm-up activity that will get all players jogging, fielding and throwing (Figure 3.1). Participating will give players an initial understanding of how the diamond is set up, which way to run and a concept of fielding and throwing to the base the base-runner is running to.

Set out as many diamonds as are needed for the number of players. Step out between 15 and 18 steps between cones. For this first activity ten players per diamond works well. Start with three in a line, one behind the other in the traditional shortstop position (between second and third base). Have a player stand at first base with another two players standing behind that base. The remainder players line up as in a normal batting line behind home plate. The first 'batter' throws the ball to the player at the front of the shortstop line then jogs towards first base not attempting to beat the throw to first base. The batters

Developing Thinking Players 27

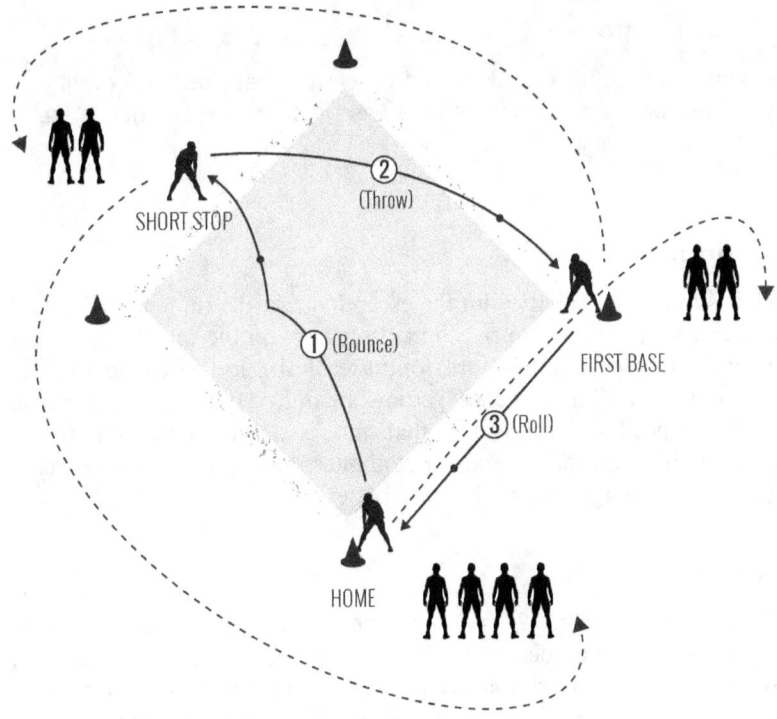

Figure 3.1 Warmup activity one.
Source: Reprinted from *Developing Thinking Players: Teaching baseball and softball through modified games and activities.* Image used with permission from ETNZ Ltd.

throw must be one bounce and directly to the fielder. This is the time to reinforce with all players that the activities at this stage are not about 'beating' the fielding team but making it easy for the fielders to field the ball. The shortstop fields the ball and throws the ball, on the full, to the player on first base. If they are not able to throw the full distance, they take a few steps towards first base until they are close enough for their throw to reach the fielder on the full. The runner jogs through first base and then joins the back of the first base line – the fielder at first base rolls the ball back to home plate, jogs around behind second base and joins the back of the shortstop line. The shortstop who fielded the ball jogs behind third base to the back of the batting line. The next player, in both the shortstop and first base line, steps forward to play the position. Use two or three balls and keep the activity moving freely.

> **Rule to introduce**
>
> Forced run: If a runner is forced to run to a base they are out if a fielder, who has contact with the base, catches the ball before the runner reaches it.

Activity two

This is the same activity with the exception that the runner runs at half to three-quarters pace to put limited pressure on the throw. The intent is for the throw from the short stop to reach the first base fielder before the runner gets there, hence getting an out. At this point you will probably need to reemphasis that this is about giving the fielder opportunities to practice and is not about throwing in such a way as to gain an advantage for the thrower (batter).

Activity three

This activity (Figure 3.2) is designed to give fielders an opportunity to experience a limited degree of decision-making in a game-like context. At this stage, the decision-making is restricted to the shortstop deciding whether to throw to first or second base. While this may seem reasonably simple, it does offer an introduction to the concept of risk and reward. Is it better to throw to second base with the reward of getting the lead runner out but with the risk that if the out is missed, this will leave two runners on base without an out? Would it be a better decision to throw to first base where there is a higher chance of getting an out? (Doing so, however, leaves a player in scoring position on second base.)

Factors that may influence the shortstops decision of whether to throw to first or second include:

1 how cleanly the ball was fielded;
2 the strength of throw required;
3 the speed of the runner(s) and how close to second base the runner is;
4 whether the fielder who is covering second base is in a good position to take the out; and
5 the speed of the ball being fielded.

In this play, the second base fielder must run to cover second base to receive the throw. As the outs at both first and second base are forced

Developing Thinking Players 29

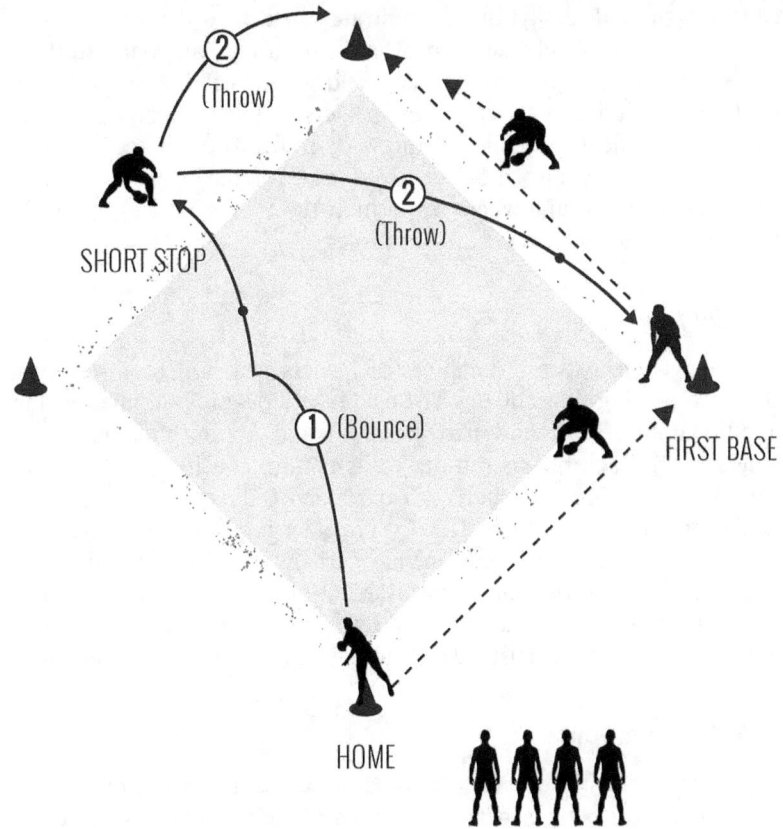

Figure 3.2 Activity three.
Source: Reprinted from *Developing Thinking Players: Teaching baseball and softball through modified games and activities.* Image used with permission from ETNZ Ltd.

plays no tag is required. Again, the thrower (batter) throws directly to shortstop.

After the play is completed the runner who ran to second base rejoins the batting team, and the runner who ran to first base stays as a base runner on first. This configuration is repeated each time the activity is reset, independent of the results of the play. Leave the fielders in position for five to ten plays and then rotate players as suits.

To increase the complexity of this activity, introduce the option of throwing to either the second base fielder *or* the shortstop. Again, this must be a single bounce directly to the fielder to ensure that the fielder can field the ball easily and concentrate on tactical decision-making. Both fielders need to be aware of what to do if the ball comes to them and what to do if it goes to the other fielder. This will increase the level of decision-making required for the fielders as there are now two possible actions, field the ball and throw or move to cover second base. The single bounce also introduces the need for the batter to start to think tactically around where to position the throw. Rotate players so that they all experience the different roles.

Activity four

This activity increases the number of fielders who will be involved in decision- making substantially. The field is set up with four infielders (an additional fielder at third base position) and a runner on first base (Figure 3.3). Each play is run out to its natural conclusion. The batter can choose to throw the ball (still one bounce directly to the selected fielder) to any of the four fielders. Every fielder needs to know what they will do if the ball is thrown to them, or to any of the other fielders. An example of a question that can be asked of players: If the ball is thrown to shortstop what will I do? If it is thrown to the third base fielder what will I do (each fielder must either field the ball or cover an empty base)?

> **Rule to introduce**
>
> Non-forced run: If a runner makes a choice to attempt to run to a base they are out if a fielder catches the ball and can tag the runner, when they are not touching a base, with a hand/glove that holds the ball. The fielder does not need to have contact with the base at the time of tagging. This includes a runner who has run past second or third base and can therefore be tagged out.

Considering tactics for the fielding team, during every play, all four bases must be covered by a fielder. An example of a question that can be asked of players: If you are not the person fielding the ball (you must be moving to cover a base) are you thinking about what you will do before it happens?

This activity is a time to further develop the understanding that tactical decision-making is important for the batting team as well as the fielding team. An example of a question that can be asked of players: Looking at the situation in the field which is the best fielder for

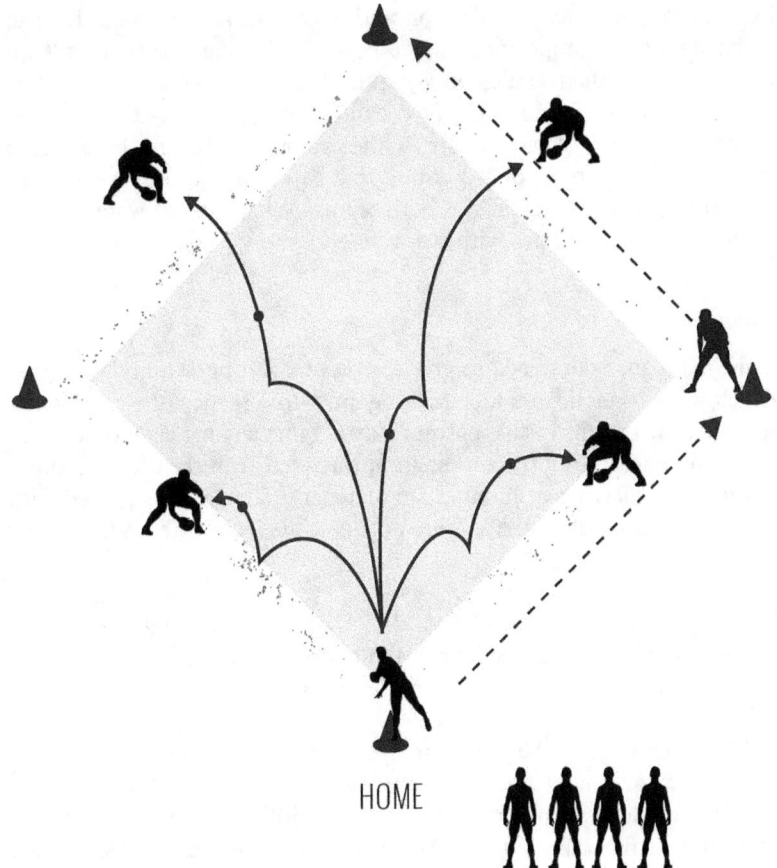

Figure 3.3 Activity four.
Source: Reprinted from *Developing Thinking Players: Teaching baseball and softball through modified games and activities.* Image used with permission from ETNZ Ltd.

them to throw the ball to (Get them to discuss their options and the positives and negatives of each)?

In activity four (Figure 3.3), the play continues until it reaches its natural conclusion. If the runner to second base, for example, makes it successfully (s)he may decide to take a risk and try to run to third base and the fielding team should respond appropriately. In some cases, the play can end with a run being scored. This is often the result of a player making an initial error and then making a second error trying to compensate for the first. At the end of the play the players should have the opportunity to reflect on and discuss what happened. During activity four, it is important to give both the fielding and batting team time to discuss their tactics on a regular basis.

Options for variation in the field can be set up any way the coach or players wish. For example, start with a runner on second base rather than first. An example of a question that can be asked of players: How does that change the tactics of both teams? What if there were runners on first and second base with two outs?

Game one

This first game is designed to give the players an opportunity to further develop their tactical understanding and to practice their decision-making. Two teams of five players play a game against each other with the fielding team set up as in diagram three but with the addition of an extra fielder playing at home plate (catcher). The game is played with the normal rules of softball, three outs and the team is retired, etc. The only exceptions are that:

- the ball must still be thrown directly to a fielder (one bounce). If the throw is too difficult then the batter is out; and
- no short throws equivalent to a bunt allowed.

While the rules of the game are like those of softball or baseball, the game and equipment are again modified to allow the players to successfully implement their decision-making without being restricted by a lack of specific skill(s). Tactical considerations may be focussed by a central question that the fielding team needs to answer: 'What happens if … and what will I do?' Players therefore need to:

1 Communicate clearly with each other before and during the play.
2 Consider what the batting team would like to achieve? Can this be counteracted through your tactics?
3 Be aware of the potential effects of pressure and think through how you will manage it. Don't rush, take it one step at a time, field cleanly then throw.
4 Throw accurately with sufficient speed to achieve the out. *Don't* throw fast just because you can. Consider the fielder's ability to catch and the distance between the thrower and the catcher.
5 When making decisions it is important to understand, and consider, the potential reward if it goes well and the risk should something go wrong.

Developing Thinking Players

At the same time, the batting/throwing team needs to consider the same factors in deciding which fielder to throw to. Throwing to the third base fielder with a force run to home and no outs would not, for example, be a good choice. In all discussions both the batting and fielding teams need to factor in such things as ... how many out ... which runners are forced to run ... the score ... what the innings is.

Game two: Softball Sense

The game 'Softball Sense' is a progression from the first game and offers players the opportunity to practice implementing the tactical decision-making developed in previous activities in a game that more closely resembles the 'real' game of baseball/softball.

Rules of Softball Sense:

1. In field only ... six fielders including player standing in pitcher's position.
2. Batters bat of a batting tee. Use a ball appropriate for the skill level of players; a soft, softball sized ball can be used if fielders lack confidence.
3. Some strong batters can be required to bat on their non-dominant side.
4. Ball hit into outfield on full ... batter is out.
5. Ball hit through infield to the outfield ... all runners two bases.
6. All other normal rules of softball followed.

> **Rules to introduce**
>
> Ball caught on the full: batter is out. If a baserunner is off the base when the ball is caught they must return to the base they have just left. If the ball is caught by a fielder in contact with this base before they get back to it they are also out ... no tag needed as they are forced to return. If the runner stays on the base until the ball is caught they can decide whether to try to run to the next base. They cannot leave the base until the moment it is caught and as it is non-forced, they need to be tagged to be put out.

Other game options

The above activities and games can be further modified as suits the needs of the group. The softball sense game can be played with a pitcher pitching the ball, but this must be done in a way that maintains the game as a hitting/ fielding game. Two options are to have a member of the batting team pitch to their own team members or to select a pitcher who can pitch strikes at a pace that the batters can hit regularly.

Conclusion

The context of baseball/softball has been used in this chapter to illustrate the DTP^{TM} approach. It is, however, an approach to teaching and coaching that can be applied across many other sports and games. I have used this approach in sports such as volleyball, for example, where in the initial stages players are able to catch and throw the ball up for spikers rather than using a dig and set. This allows the players to concentrate on court movement and quite advanced tactics. Enjoy.

References

Araújo, D., Hristovski, R., Seifert, L., Carvalho, J. & Davids, K. (2019). Ecological cognition: expert decision-making behaviour in sport. *International Review of Sport and Exercise Psychology*, 12(1), 1–25.

Bunker, D. & Thorpe, R. (1982). A model for the teaching of games in the secondary school. *Bulletin of Physical Education*, 18(1), 5–8.

Gordon, B. (2015). *Developing Thinking Players: Baseball/softball edition*. Wellington, New Zealand: ETNZ.

Harvey, S., Cope, E. & Jones, R. (2016). Developing questioning in game-centred approaches. *Journal of Physical Education, Recreation and Dance*, 87, 28–35.

Harvey, S. & Light, R. (2015). Questioning for learning in game-based approaches to teaching and coaching. *Asia Pacific Journal of Health, Sport and Physical Education*, 6(2), 175–190.

Konings, M. & Hettinga, F. (2018). Pacing decision making in sport and the effects of interpersonal competition: A critical review. *Journal of Sports Medicine*, 48(8), 1829–1843.

Pate, R. (2012). Open versus closed questions: What constitutes a good question? In E. Ortlieb & R. Bowden (eds), *Educational research and innovations* (pp. 29–39). CEDER.

Turner, A. (2018). Athlete-centred coaching and teaching games for understanding. In S. Pill (ed.), *Perspectives on athlete-centred coaching*. (pp. 127–136). New York: Routledge.

4 'Because we're here lad, and nobody else. Just us.'[1]

An existential–phenomenological perspective on game-based approaches

Ruan Jones and David Piggott

> I don't believe it! I don't believe it! I do not believe it! Bobby Thomson hit a line drive into the lower deck of the left-field stands and this place is goin' crazy! The Giants! Horace Stoneham has got a winner! The Giants won it by a score of 5 to 4, and they're pickin' Bobby Thomson up, and carryin' him off the field!

This commentary, by Russ Hodges of WMCA-AM radio, immortalises probably the most famous moment in baseball history: a 'shot heard round the world'.[2] It is a description of Bobby Thompson's game-winning home run for the New York Giants off Brooklyn Dodgers pitcher Ralph Branca at the Polo Grounds in New York City on 3 October 1951. With it, they won the National League pennant. Thomson's dramatic three-run homer came in the ninth and final innings of the decisive third game of a three-game playoff in which the Giants trailed by 4 runs to 2. What makes this game even more remarkable is the narrative underlying the play-off series. Naturally the intense and historic cross-town rivalry in the first instance, but also the dramatic last few weeks of the regular season. In mid-August, the Giants were 13½ games behind the league-leading Dodgers and they won 37 of their final 44 games to tie Brooklyn on the final day of the regular season, to force the play-off.

This anecdote, at one level, may remind us of the reasons why we cherish sport so much. For example:

- the drama of the nail-biting finish and awe-inspiring home-run;
- the excruciating uncertainty of the contest;
- the absurdity at how the entire season comes down to the ninth and final innings of the final play-off game;
- the anxiety as Branca pitches that final ball to Thompson; and
- the contrasting joy, relief and despair at the conclusion of the contest.

Yet, at a deeper level, it provides a metaphor for our very existence as human beings. It is precisely the contention that sport is an existential contest that will provide the focus of this chapter. If sport is a microcosm of existence, then it follows that how we structure practice environments must take account of this. Specifically, we will discuss how existential philosophy can contribute and enhance our understanding of game-based approaches (GBA) in coaching contexts by drawing on the work of Martin Heidegger (1927) and Peter Arnold (1979). We will also argue the case for an existential–phenomenological research agenda that explores the lived meaning of athletes when coached through the medium of a GBA.

The interest in GBA within the coaching literature has made great advances in recent years. There is a sufficient body of evidence to warrant a recent review (Kinnerk, Harvey, MacDonncha & Lyons, 2018), and of particular interest to us is the work on the theoretical and applied nature of *Positive Pedagogy* (PP) (Light & Harvey, 2017, 2019). PP is an umbrella term that encapsulates a collection of philosophical, theoretical and pedagogical characteristics, the aim of which are to provide a self-determined environment, empowering athletes to make intelligent and creative decisions and encouraging self-expression and human growth. It is not as Light (2019) emphasises a model or blueprint.

As long-standing proponents of Teaching Games for Understanding (TGFU: Bunker and Thorpe, 1982) and other GBAs, we wholeheartedly agree with many of the foundations upon which PP sits, of which Game Sense (den Duyn, 1997) is one. There is also no doubt that PP is built on solid holistic foundations. For example, the theory of embodied cognition that Light and colleagues argue underpin GBAs (Light & Fawns, 2003, 2010; Light, Harvey & Mouchet, 2014). These authors, for example, disavow dualist epistemological thought that consider mind and body as separate 'things'. Notwithstanding this, we diverge in our view of some of the Humanistic philosophical principles that PP sits upon.

Before we start to outline the contrasting perspectives of Humanism and Existentialism, we wish to emphasise that this *is not* a criticism of PP; there will be no straw-man construction here, indeed, as Nesti (2005) explains, the differences are relatively few, yet nuanced and profound. Rather, we provide a well-meaning discourse on how some of the characteristics of existential philosophy, and, in turn existential–phenomenological research can (a) inform and add value to the coach–athlete world, and (b) help us to structure meaningful GBA coaching scenarios. As such, this chapter should be read and interpreted in the collegial spirit it which it is intended.

Humanism and existentialism

Humanists espouse the goal of becoming a fully-functioning person through a process of self-growth and self-fulfilment:

> Less and less does [the individual] look to others for approval or disapproval, for standards to live by; for decisions and choices. [The individual] recognises that it rests within him [or her] self to choose; that the only question which matters is, 'Am I living in a way which is deeply satisfying to me, and which truly expresses me'? This is I think perhaps the most important question for the creative individual.
>
> (Rogers, 1995a, p. 119)

In this passage Rogers, establishes the common ground that Humanism shares with Existentialism, and the point of departure. Both Humanism and Existentialism share the view that to live an authentic life is of paramount importance. Living authentically means that as human beings, we are always faced with the responsibility of choice and making choices that are clearly consistent with our own values and beliefs. Rogers (1995a, 1995b) cites, existential philosopher, Soren Kierkegaard, in recognition of their shared interpretation of the dilemma that an individual may face.

The point of departure lies in the Humanistic contention that authenticity – a philosophical antecedent of autonomy – is necessary as part of the journey of achieving the *Actualising Tendency* (Nesti, 2005; Spinelli, 1989); a phrase coined by Rogers (1995a, 1995b) to describe a human striving to achieve the ideal self. According to existential therapists, it follows that any philosophy that emphasises and encourages the actualising tendency of the individual may come at the expense of 'others' subjective experiences' (Spinelli, 1989, p. 160). Within the current coaching literature this very issue has been raised as a dilemma, as Bowles and O'Dwyer observe succinctly:

> The maintenance of an ACA [Athlete Centred Approach] within a team environment challenged us. We were prompted to reflect on how to remain focused on individual players' needs while we also worked on building an effective team. We were very aware that some team decisions impact adversely on individual players. These challenges presented in a team environment were more apparent in the closing stages of the season when team selections, tactics and strategies became more important. Over the course of the season,

our coach reflections sought to tease out the apparent contradictions between being athlete-centred and team-centred.

(Bowles & O'Dwyer, 2019, pp. 15–16)

Existential proponents do not, therefore, have an issue with freedom *per se*, but rather the idea that freedom can be absolute. Instead, they argue in favour of contingent or situated freedom (Dale, 1996; Fahlberg, Fahlberg & Gates, 1992; Nesti, 2005). This idea of situated freedom is most frequently expressed through *being-in-the-world* (Heidegger, 1927).

Martin Heidegger (1889–1976) was a German philosopher, whose work was readily associated with existentialism and the phenomenological method. Phenomenology is a philosophical approach to the study of human experience and the way things, or objects of consciousness, appear through such experience (Sokolowski, 2000). Heidegger was interested in the very existence of human being, and what it meant to be a being! It was his belief that a human being (using the phraseology 'Dasein') is an individual but also part of the world shared with others who may have different languages, cultures, values, expectations and prior knowledge (Heidegger, 1927). These differences can exert constraints upon what is permissible within a community, and yet the person also has the freedom to act upon the world, to define and choose their future, subject to the constraints in which they were 'thrown' (termed *geworfen* in German) into the world with. Individuals who accept their responsibility as existent beings to make choices in their lives are said to be living authentic lives despite often experiencing anxiety and alienation from their community: this may be the price of authentic existence. To resist the hard and difficult choice is to follow Das Man (the 'they'): 'The "they" of which he speaks [Heidegger] denies true existence in that it takes away choice and disburdens the individual of responsibility' (Arnold, 1979, p. 40). Anxiety and alienation are two recurring themes of discussion for existential therapists (Nesti, 2005; Spinelli, 1989; Yalom, 1980).

If we return to the reflections on the difficulty of reconciling the athlete's autonomy within the team (Bowles & O'Dwyer, 2019); from an existential perspective the athlete does indeed have the freedom to choose how to behave, but this freedom is: (a) situated within the context of the team environment that s/he is 'thrown'; and (b) coupled with the responsibility that making a choice entails. Responsibility from this perspective does not have ethical or moral connotations (i.e. there is no 'right' or 'wrong', 'good' or 'bad' choice, but there is *always* a choice that must be made). There is one final point we wish to make before we discuss how Heidegger's phenomenological project might affect practice design with GBAs. Heidegger (1927) in his analysis cleverly establishes the holistic nature of Dasein (literally translated as 'Being-there') for it at once confirms the existential and subjective nature of our Being, and yet locates our Being in a setting or context as an empirical object (Yalom, 1980).

The case for existential–phenomenological research in GBAs

Research within coaching contexts have typically taken dual-epistemological perspectives. Traditions of research that stem from positivist and interpretivist paradigms succeed in abstracting human experience from the context of the world in which they are situated. Existential phenomenological research traditions proceed from the *a priori* assumption that Dasein is being-in-the world. From this starting point, therefore, the athlete's relationships with others cannot be discounted. Despite its rich philosophical heritage there is a very practical question that ties us all to the coaching community: 'What does it mean to be an athlete in the world?' Reductionist methods that reduce athlete experience to *the what* of coaching cannot answer this; likewise, interpretation is 'the interpretation [of behaviour] put upon the [athlete] by others' (Arnold, 1979, p. 15). The best person to help us understand the athlete is the athlete themselves (Chronin & Armour, 2017).

We are under no illusion that an attempt to articulate existential philosophy and the accompanying phenomenological method in such an abridged format, is an extremely difficult task. There is, however, an emerging tradition of existential phenomenological advocacy and research within physical education, coaching and the movement sciences more broadly (Allen-Collinson, 2009; Brown & Payne, 2009; Gearity, 2012; Jones, Harvey & Kirk, 2016). Chronin & Armour (2015, 2017) advocated for phenomenological research approaches (existential among them) in a series of studies on the lived experiences and lived meaning of community and youth performance coaches. Within the narratives that they formed to represent their findings, they explored the importance of the hidden organisational world of community coaching that is frequently in stark contrast to the public image, but also the intersubjective nature of the coaching world and the complex relationships that exist with the 'other'. Further to our earlier point, the findings of Chronin & Armour (2015, 2017) clearly hint at the situated constraints of being-in-the-world, that the coach will experience. Their research resonates with Kinnerk et al.'s (2018) recommendation for further examination of the less formal coach settings – in other words a more interconnected exploration of the coach–athlete setting that existential phenomenological research is able to take account of. In the next section we will flesh out how Heidegger's ontological phenomenological project shape the way that GBA practice can be viewed.

Immersive game-based narratives

We propose a theoretical conception of a GBA practice scenarios based upon existential–phenomenological principles in which the athlete is viewed as 'being-in-the-world' (Heidegger, 1927, h53). From this perspective, the athlete, their environment, and any number of past experiences, are indissoluble or co-constituted (Fahlberg, Fahlberg & Gates, 1992, Spinelli, 1989). In terms of the construction of these practice scenarios, which we popularise as immersive game-based narratives (IGNs), a number of factors must be considered when determining their construction. These include, for example:

- the vicarious and lived experiences of athletes (the sights, sounds, emotions, feelings, and thoughts of sporting contests past – either directly or vicariously experienced);
- their meaning in the lives of athletes;
- their problem-based nature;
- their 'representative' nature; and
- the risk and reward that these IGNs must take account of.

Athletes are thrown into counter-factual ('what-if') conditioned situations. These immersive and often chaotic game simulations attempt to replicate the conditions that an athlete has experienced directly or indirectly. The use of the phraseology – 'narrative' – is deliberate because it intones the chronicling of interconnected events in the lives of an athlete or athletes. In this respect, not spoken or written, but lived.

It is evident that other scenario-based models are already used in coaching settings: for example, Designer Games (Charlesworth, 1974), Action Fantasy (Launder, 2001) and Affective Learning Design (Headrick, Renshaw, Davids, Pinder & Araujo, 2019). The virtue of Action Fantasy games is extolled by Jones et al. (2016). In relation to the Designer Game (Charlesworth, 1974), insofar as he refers to the 'tactical, technical, psychological, competitive and physical' (p. 30) demands, these are undisputed. However, looking at Designer Games (DGs) through an existential–phenomenological lens, being is explored as an empirical phenomenon.

The demands to which Charlesworth refers, therefore, are objective characteristics of a skilful performer within a GBA and serve to situate the athlete within the world. All the respective phenomena described can be measured, be it levels of anxiety, mood state, physiological measures of performance or decision-making capabilities. What DGs would appear to lack are those moments that truly stand out as personally meaningful in an athlete's existence. These situations have meaning as existential movement (Arnold, 1979).

Let us refer to the anecdote in which we started the chapter. Bobby Thompson stands at the batting plate, bottom of the ninth innings. Months of the regular and play-off season have come to this. Factor in that these are the first televised games in baseball history - millions watching nationwide. There are a multitude of objective considerations in that moment that the DG approach would attempt to prepare Thompson for, but one it doesn't: Thompson might well ask himself the questions: '*Why me?*' and '*Why now?*'. He would be justified in doing so because humans are rational creatures that justifiably seek meaning and answers to questions when they find themselves in situations such as the one described. The Existentialist answers: There is no sense to this, it is absurd, ridiculous – *there's no meaning* – accept the situation. In accepting the absurdity of the situation, '… the existent is able to take possession of himself and live in accordance with his choices and decisions' (Arnold, 1979, p. 40). At this moment human being finds itself as authentic. Thompson strikes the home run and the Giants win.

These IGNs, in which athletes are figuratively thrown into and told to 'get yourself out of that' give greater meaning to GBA structured practices because they are viewed as reality and not just any conditioned game that is divorced from the athlete's existence. Most recently, Headrick et al. (2019) begun to explore the role that emotions can play in their discussion of Affective Learning Design (ALD), in the context of non-linear pedagogy. This we argue, is a very important development in sports coaching and provides evidence that the affective learning domain needs considerably greater attention. Emotions clearly impact upon decision-making in all sport settings (Tenenbaum, Basevitch, Gershgoren & Filho, 2013) and the relationship between affect and cognition has long been of interest in cognitive psychology (e.g. Forgas, 2000, 2008). We call for a shift from *knowing* the effect that emotions play within GBA settings to exploring *being* when emotions overtake athletes in highly pressurised situations. The intention being, to understand how athletes make sense of, and utilise, emotions.

Concluding remarks

Proponents of existential–phenomenological principles within GBA settings would contend that the athlete is 'thrown' into chaotic situations that are often difficult to rationalise and make sense of. Within these situations the 'authentic' athlete accepts the absurdity and the lack of sense, with the responsibility and determination to make a choice. In contrast to positive psychology – underpinned by Humanist philosophy – there is no actualising tendency or personal growth that accompanies the responsibility of personal choice, for freedom is not absolute but contingent upon our being-in-the-world. It is in this respect that our views contrast with proponents of PP (Light & Harvey, 2017, 2019). Thinking in this way requires a dramatic shift in the way we come to view the coach–athlete relationship.

Heidegger's existential–phenomenological project is ontological, because of the attempt to uncover the meaning of being at any given time and in any given moment. It is not to know 'what' a phenomenon is (that falls within the positivist paradigm) or interpret why athletes may behave or perform in a certain way in relation to a phenomenon (interpretivism). Instead, an existential–phenomenological researcher asks: 'How do athletes makes sense of their lives within a specific moment?' 'What is the meaning of this phenomenon when an athlete makes decisions, experiences emotions and relates to others-in-their-world?'. 'In short, action in human movement is concerned with the perspective of the performing agent' (Arnold, 1979, p. 15). The proceeding chapter provides practical coaching examples of how we have interpreted IGNs within basketball and cricket, illustrated with the existential–phenomenological foundations that have been outlined above.

Notes

1 Colour Sergeant Bourne in *Zulu* (1964). When asked 'Why is it us?' this is his reply.
2 The phrase is taken from *Concord Hymn* (1837), a poem by Ralph Waldo Emerson.

References

Allen-Collinson, J. (2009). Sporting embodiment: Sports studies and the (continuing) promise of phenomenology. *Qualitative Research in Sport and Exercise*, 1, 279–296.

Arnold, P. (1979). *Meaning and movement in sport and physical education*. London: Heinemann.

An existential–phenomenological angle 43

Bowles R. & O'Dwyer, A. (2019) Athlete-centred coaching: perspectives from the sideline. *Sports Coaching Review*, published online first.

Brown, T. D. & Payne, P. G. (2009). Conceptualizing the phenomenology of movement in physical education: Implications for pedagogical inquiry and development. *Quest*, 61, 418–441.

Bunker, D. & Thorpe, R. (1982). A model for the teaching of games in the secondary school. *Bulletin of Physical Education*, 10, 9–16.

Charlesworth, R. (1974). Designer games. *Sport Coach*, 17(4), 30–33.

Chronin, C. & Armour, K. (2015). Lived experience and community sport coaching: A phenomenological investigation. *Sport, Education and Society*, 20(8), 959–975.

Chronin, C. & Armour, K. (2017). 'Being' in the coaching world: New insights on youth performance coaching from an interpretative phenomenological approach. *Sport, Education and Society*, 22(8), 919–931.

Dale, G. (1996). Existential–phenomenology: Emphasising the experience of the athlete in sport psychology research. *The Sport Psychologist*, 10, 158–171.

den Duyn, N. (1997). *Game sense: Developing thinking players*. Canberra, ACT: Australian Sports Commission.

Fahlberg, L. L., Fahlberg L. K. & Gates, K. W. (1992). Experience and existence: exercise behaviour from an existential–phenomenological perspective. *The Sport Psychologist*, 6, 172–191.

Forgas, J. P. (2000). *Feeling and thinking: The role of affect in social cognition*. Sydney, NSW: Cambridge University Press.

Forgas, J. P. (2008). Affect and cognition. *Perspectives on Psychological Science*, 3, 94–101.

Gearity, B. T. (2012). Poor teaching by the coach: a phenomenological description from athletes' experience of poor coaching. *Physical Education and Sport Pedagogy*, 17(1), 79–96.

Headrick, J., Renshaw, I., Davids, K., Pinder, R. & Araujo, D. (2019). The dynamics of expertise acquisition in sport: The role of affective learning design. *Psychology of Sport and Exercise*, 16, 83–90.

Heidegger, M. (1927). *Being and time* (trans. J. Macquarrie & E. Robinson, 1962). London: SCM Press.

Jones, R., Harvey, S. & Kirk, D. (2016). Everything is at stake; yet nothing is at stake: Exploring meaning-making in game-centred approaches. *Sport, Education and Society*, 21(6), 888–906.

Kinnerk, P., Harvey, S., MacDonncha C. & Lyons, M. (2018). A review of the game-based approaches to coaching literature in competitive team sport settings. *Quest*, 70(4), 401–418.

Launder, A. (2001) *Play Practice*. Champaign, IL: Human Kinetics.

Light, R. & Fawns, R. (2003). Knowing the game: Integrating speech and action in games teaching through TGfU. *Quest*, 55, 161–176.

Light, R. & Fawns, R. (2010). The thinking body: Constructivist approaches to games teaching in physical education. *Critical Studies in Education*, 42(2), 69–87.

Light, R. & Harvey, S. (2017). Positive pedagogy for sport coaching. *Sport, Education and Society,* 22(2), 271–287.
Light, R. & Harvey, S. (2019) *Positive pedagogy for sport coaching* (2nd edition). London: Routledge.
Light, R., Harvey, S. & Mouchet, A. (2014). Improving 'at-action' decision-making in team sports through a holistic coaching approach. *Sport, Education and Society,* 19(3), 258–275.
Nesti, M. (2005). *Existential psychology and sport: Theory and applications.* London: Routledge.
Rogers, C. R. (1995a). *On becoming a person: A therapist's view of psychotherapy.* New York: Houghton Mifflin.
Rogers, C. R. (1995b). *A way of being.* New York: Houghton Mifflin.
Sokolowski, R. (2000). *Introduction to phenomenology.* Cambridge: Cambridge University Press.
Spinelli, E. (1989) *The interpreted world.* London: Sage.
Tenenbaum, G., Basevitch, I., Gershgoren, L. & Filho, E. (2013). Emotions-decision-making in sport: Theoretical conceptualization and experimental evidence. *International Journal of Sport and Exercise Psychology* 11(2), 151–168.
Yalom, I. (1980). *Existential psychotherapy.* New York: Basic Books.

5 The practical application of immersive game-based narratives

David Piggott and Ruan Jones

In the previous chapter we outlined the multi-layered conceptual basis for what we called Immersive Game-based Narratives (IGNs), drawing on the combined influences of TGfU, designer games, action fantasies, positive pedagogy, affective learning design and existential phenomenology. In this chapter we explore the ways in which these ideas can be combined and applied in sports coaching through two examples: one a vicarious grassroots scenario in cricket; the other a lived experience scenario in professional basketball. Through these examples we show how IGNs can be applied effectively in different coaching settings, with different game forms and with both children and adults.

Problem-based coaching from a 'game model'

In Chapter 4 we identified a series of factors to consider when designing IGNs, including: their problem-based nature; representativeness; and risk-reward considerations. To be more specific, before designing effective IGNs it is necessary to develop a deep understanding of the sport in question. This enables a coach to define the main problems that the sport presents to players which, in turn, helps them to 'represent' those problems authentically in the games and practices they design. Developing a deep understanding of the sport in question also raises awareness of the way in which those problems, played out in context, manifest as risk-reward decisions that players must learn to make to become successful in playing the game.

Developing a deep understanding of a sport is not an easy task; it often emerges over many years of experience. However, in our experience as coach developers, it can be supported and expedited by drawing on some of the ideas of the early TGfU theorists (Harvey, Pill & Almond, 2018). According to Suits (1978), understanding a game begins with the identification of the goal, the 'constitutive' (or primary) rules and how they combine to produce problems. Invasion games, for example, typically have a common goal (score more goals or points than an opposition team) and set of primary rules (e.g. a long pitch with goals at the ends; an opposition of equal number; a time limit; limits on physical contact etc.) (Almond, 1986). Through analysing the likely implications of these goal–rule–opposition interactions, it is possible to define a rough 'game model' with an attendant set of phases (or moments) and problems (Table 5.1). In this case, the rules of invasion games (e.g. pitch size and shape, time limits, number of opposition) mean that possession changes regularly from one team to another, creating distinct phases or moments of play, in and out of possession, where transition is defined as a period of time where teams are disorganised, normally a few seconds. Each phase or moment therefore has attendant problems to solve.

The more specific rules of different invasion games create different variations or emphases on each of the problems listed in Table 5.1. For example, basketball has a 24-second shot clock which means that maintaining possession for long periods is pointless; finding ways to penetrate the perimeter and interior defensive lines is the priority. The laws of the rugby forbid players from passing forwards (and enable point scoring from penalties conceded anywhere in the opposition half), hence gaining territory is arguably more important. Finally, the rules of association football force players to manipulate the ball with their feet, placing greater focus on the problem of maintaining possession than in many other invasion games. Through this more fine-grained type of analysis, it is possible to develop a specific 'game

Table 5.1 A simplified model of invasion games.

Phase/Moment	In possession	Transition	Out of possession
Problems	How do we maintain possession of the ball/puck? How do we progress the ball/puck up the pitch/court? How do we penetrate a final defensive block or line and score?	How do we take advantage of a disorganised opponent? How do we prevent the opposition from taking advantage of our disorganised state?	How do we get pressure on the ball/puck? How do we prevent the opposition from moving up the field/court? How do we prevent penetration of our defensive block or line?

model' in a given sport, defining the structure and flow of the game and also the main problems that players have to learn to solve (through the application of specialised skills and physical prowess). Considering the forthcoming examples, Figures 5.1 and 5.2 offer game models for cricket and basketball. These models have been developed and refined over many years through our own work as coaches and coach developers.

In this model of cricket (Figure 5.1), there is a single main problem at the centre: that of determining the level of risk required in each discipline (batting, bowling or fielding) in order to win the game from a specific point, based on an assessment of conditions. Elite level cricketers, according to our model, must constantly monitor the conditions (around the outside of the central circle in Figure 5.1) – their *own strengths and weaknesses* (or action capabilities), those of their *opponent*, the state of the *pitch* and *weather*, and the *state and stage of the game* – in order to select an appropriate 'risk mode' which, in turn, implies the selection of specific strategies and techniques (assuming they are available to the players). The model also suggests that the selection of 'risk modes' is interdependent with the opposition.

Let us suppose, for example, that the batting team is severely behind in a run chase, that the pitch and weather conditions are flat and benign, and that the opposition have just brought on a part-time bowler. The batting team would likely select a very high 'risk mode' and mobilise their biggest hits and riskiest running strategies, trying to turn every single run into two or more runs. The fielding team would therefore likely select a low 'risk mode', bowling with high accuracy organising deep, spread-out field settings in order to limit the scoring (hence the opposite shading on the arrows on the ball in the centre of Figure 5.1).

Although this model is quite different to those that typically break the game into disciplinary and technique-based categories (e.g. Mitchell, Oslin & Griffin, 2013) we have found that the model resonates well with experienced cricket coaches who recognise that the best players not only have a wide range of techniques, *but also* the ability to select the right technique at the right moment. If we accept this way of understanding the game, the next question is: how early in a child's development can you start to present these types of complex risk-reward decision-making problems? And what types of games and activities might we use to invite young players into this way of thinking and playing? We return to these questions following the introduction of a game model of basketball.

Basketball is a specific type of invasion game that is heavily governed by rules that force a team to get the ball forward and take shots

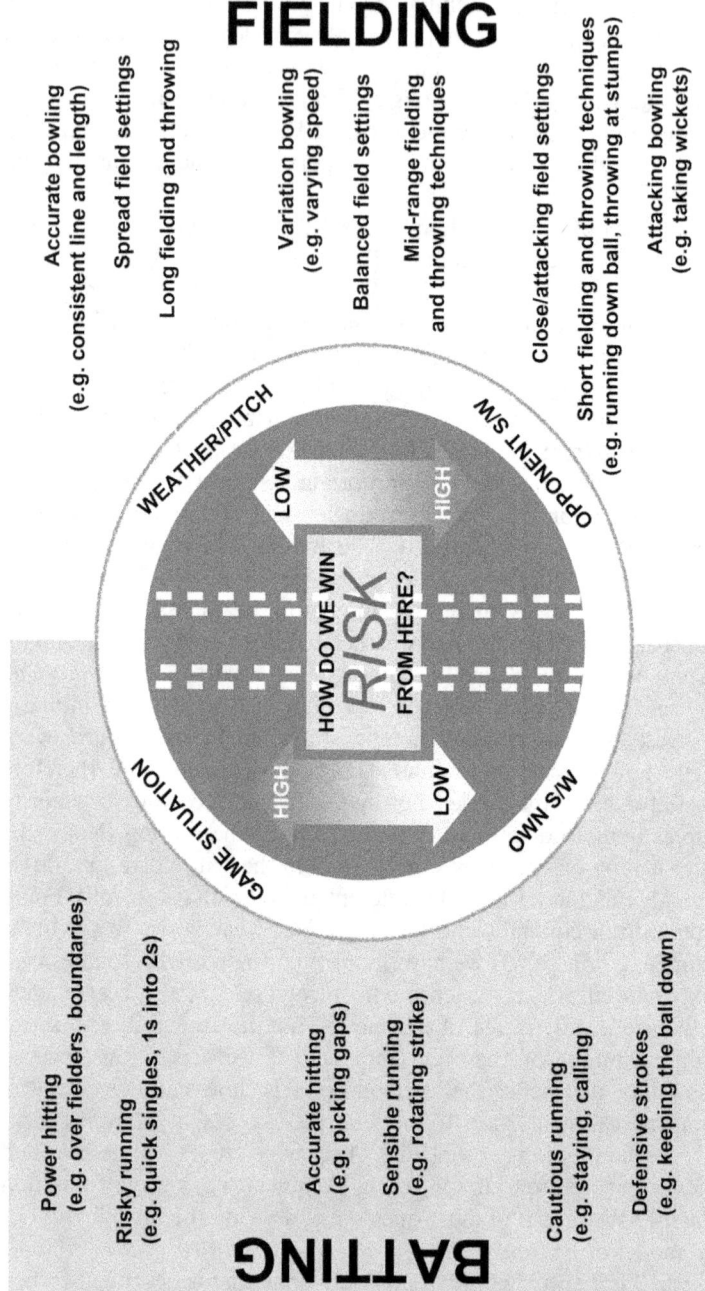

Figure 5.1 A game model of cricket.

quickly. In addition to the 24-second shot clock, there are also '8-second' and 'back-court' rules that force the offensive team to get the ball over the half quickly and to keep it there. Hence, whilst our model of basketball has the hallmarks of many invasion game models, with in/out of possession and transition phases (e.g. Mitchell et al., 2013; Tee et al., 2018), the transition phase is arguably more important (and relatively longer, as a percentage of overall possession), and the problems must be solved in specific periods of time.

Again, the problems are similar to those in Table 5.1, and displayed against the mirror image of opposing problems, with more basketball specific language overlaid. For example, having advanced the ball up the court (perhaps via a fast break) and created sufficient disruption in the defensive structure, a team must find a way to take the highest value shot possible. We use the term 'high value' because, for many teams at an elite level, an open three-point shot will result in more 'points per possession' than an open two-point shot, even when very close to the basket. Teams therefore have to work out what is a 'high value' shot for them, given the skills of their players and the opposition.

This idea of developing a 'simplified vision of the whole game' was introduced into the TGfU canon via Jerome Bruner. In Bruner's view – one adopted by Len Almond (Harvey et al., 2018) – learning in any domain would be enhanced by first determining what is 'judged critical' in that subject and then introducing it 'as early as possible, in a manner consistent with a child's forms of thought' before repeating and developing the same themes over and over as the child develops (Bruner, 1960, p. 54). Developing such a game model represents the first step of this pedagogical process as it defines what is judged critical in the sport (i.e. the necessary components of the activity that must be learned in order to be effective in playing the game at the highest level). Effective coaching, then, requires that problems be represented authentically and in simplified form to a child, then developed in line with the growth of the child's physical, technical and cognitive capabilities, right into adulthood. As Bruner (1966, p. 35) wrote:

> A curriculum should involve the mastery of skills that in turn lead to the mastery of still more powerful ones, the establishment of self-reward sequences ... The reward of deeper understanding is a more robust lure to effort than we have yet realised.

Defining the main problems of a sport and finding ways to represent them appropriately for the stage of development is therefore the first step in developing a curriculum. A coach must also consider the skills that need to be mastered to solve each version of the problems as they grow in complexity. The model therefore begins to outline the tactical and technical pillars around which a curriculum can form and from which the 'mastery and self-reward sequences' can begin to create a 'lure' to the exploration of deeper levels of learning. In the next section to use these models and the associated curricula to contextualise and introduce two specific examples of IGNs, where various pedagogical and philosophical principles combine and come to life.

'Layering' the coaching experience using IGNs

The foundational conceptual 'layer' informing our IGN approach has now been established: the TGfU principles of whole-sport models, defining fundamental tactical problems, and representing these problems in simplified ways, appropriate to the level of the learner in a spiral curriculum. This set of ideas provides a macro context for the delivery of long-term sport coaching programmes. We now want to zoom into the micro level of a single session or series of sessions, necessitating the brief elucidation of two additional 'layers' of pedagogical principles.

First, we note that the classic TGfU pedagogical principle of 'representation' itself can be framed in multiple ways (Serra-Olivares, Garcia-Lopez & Calderon, 2016). We would argue that effective modified games can be 'representative' in three different ways: (1) they *represent* the basic structure of the sport (e.g. an invasion game has a direction of play and an opposition); (2) they *represent* the authentic game problems (e.g. how to move the ball up the court against an organised opponent?); and (3) they *represent* authentic contextual information (i.e. game should always have a time-frame, a score and consequences for winning and losing).

Second, and related to point 3 above, with a more representative context comes *emotion*. When a game *feels* authentic to the players, when the outcome matters deeply, and when players are invested in the self-reward sequences Bruner described, games can evoke strong emotional connections and responses. Again, this affective dimension of games coaching is not a novel idea and has been explored by Headrick and colleagues (Headrick et al., 2016). We agree with them that emotions are important since they influence the perceptions and actions of players, both positively (e.g. 'flow' states) and negatively (e.g. anxiety-induced perceptual narrowing). However, as was explained in the previous chapter, drawing on existential phenomenological ideas, our IGN approach also expands on this rather narrow framing of the emotional dimension of learning by focussing on the rich lived (or vicarious) experience of the players and the meaning of the sporting contest in their lives. In IGNs players are 'thrown' (*geworfen*) back into the rich and evocative narratives that sport can generate and, in doing so, helping them to make sense of the situations in which they find themselves.

A vicarious experience in grassroots cricket

> It was growing dark in the early evening of 24 June 2014 as England were nearing a miraculous escape in the final test against Sri Lanka at Headingley (Leeds, England). The series score was 0–0, so the victor would take the series. The final two batsmen in the middle were Moeen Ali and the number eleven, James Anderson. Together Ali and Anderson had managed to see off 20 overs of 'hostile' bowling on a decaying pitch. Ali was well set, having reached his first test century earlier (108 runs from 281 balls); Anderson had not scored but had defended 54 balls with dogged determination. There was one over remaining. Anderson was at the crease. All he had to do was survive. On the penultimate ball of the match, Anderson flailed at a short delivery from Eranga, clipping ball into the air for what seemed like minutes, before falling into the hands of Herath. Out! The Sri Lankans peeled away, ecstatic. Anderson slumped onto his bat, head in hands. He later cried through the post-match interview. In the crowd that day at Headingley was an U11 boys' cricket team from a nearby village. They, too, left the game with their heads in their hands and tears in their eyes.

As a coach on this grassroots team at Headingley this day, how could we draw on such an experience through an IGN approach? First, we would connect with the broader curriculum of the club, based on the game model (Figure 5.1). Clearly, in this scenario, England had selected a super low 'risk mode', with Anderson defending every ball. Sri Lanka were in super high 'risk mode', bowling short balls with a suffocating close field. We would therefore want to raise the players' awareness of this and then recreate the situation as closely as possible. We would play a series of small-sided (perhaps 6-a-side on a mini pitch) 'replay' type games, throwing the players right back into the situation they experienced vicariously: the final three overs of the match. This could entail the following:

- having a scoreboard with the exact score recreated for the overs;
- the exact same initial field settings and two bowlers capable of bowling similar balls;

- an attempt to mimic the effects of the pitch and weather conditions, such as a modified ball that swings or spins, or mats laid on parts of the pitch; and
- some clear consequences for the players for winning and losing (e.g. the winning team on each 'replay' game receive a point, with the overall winners receiving a reward).

We would begin each game asking questions about players' memories of the event: what they saw and heard; what they felt as each ball was bowled; how they thought Anderson and Ali must have felt; what they think the two batsmen might have said to one another in the middle; what adjustments the Sri Lankan captain was making etc. Each replay game, in effect, a new opportunity to *feel* the pressure again; the excitement and the dread; the despair and the elation.

In addition to evoking an emotional connection, each of these questions also presents an opportunity to explore the players' awareness of the conditions. Are they aware of the score? Are they aware of the bowler's strengths? What do they *feel* are their own strengths against that bowler in that moment? Are they aware of the simulated pitch and weather conditions? (note: each new question adds a new layer of complexity to the risk-reward decision at hand, so we would be very careful not to overload young players with too much information). The games afford the players an opportunity to play out different 'risk mode' choices, in response to their assessments of the conditions, with the attendant selection and execution of appropriate techniques (which we may, of course, drop into skill-based practice in order to develop). They also create opportunities to explore emotions and responses and the meaning that young people attach to them in the moment. After all, it is surely the existential experience of such moments that keeps them coming back!

A lived experience in professional basketball

> *I could barely hear my own voice above the deafening crowd, crammed into the Lightning Arena on a bouncing Friday evening. There was 4:21 remaining in the fourth quarter and, beyond my wildest expectations, we were up 82–70 to the league-leading Hawks. But as the players jogged in for the timeout and huddled around me, bent at the waist, hands on knees, I looked into their faces and knew that we were going to lose. Sure, the Hawks were the reigning champs and we were struggling in the bottom half of the table. They had the MVP and a bunch of veteran serial winners; we had a bunch of talented rookies and a coach in his first season. But you should never lose from that position! Yet, as the minutes ticked*

down, it became harder and harder to score. It was as if the basket was shrinking and the ball had become a time bomb: nobody on our team wanted to touch it. The Hawks began to turn the screws, their MVP consistently driving into the paint, drawing fouls, getting to the line and hitting 'miracle' shots. It felt inevitable. And as the buzzer finally sounded, we looked up at the scoreboard, blinking in disbelief at the bright red lights displaying the final score: 85–90. The crowd were shuffling silently to the exits. How on earth did we lose?

As the coach of this team in this real-life narrative (we are using pseudonyms here, of course) I, the first author, can briefly explain how I used the IGN approach in the practices that followed. First, given that this was a professional team, we had 3–4 practices each week with a squad of 15 players, so there was ample opportunity to explore the situation in depth. I also had the luxury of video analysis to refer to the game, play-by-play, unpicking in slow motion those fateful final four minutes. Based on this analysis I made two main observations: (1) the specific game problem (see Figure 5.2) we struggled with was 'disrupting the defence', mainly because we were not initiating our own offensive system as planned; and (2) this was largely the responsibility of our point guard, 'Rick' who looked tentative in his movements and kept glancing at the bench, as if seeking guidance.

In the first post-game practice, I presented the situation back to the players 'head-on': I began by explaining how *I felt*, and why I felt we were going to lose; I asked how they felt and, if it was similar to me, why; we talked about their emotions, play-by-play, and what effect this had on their play: how they tightened-up, how they forgot the game plan, how they became increasingly frustrated and angry, and how this led to fouls and a loss of control. I was particularly interested in Rick's response, given his 'court captain' status. Rick was initially quiet and avoidant, so I decided to 'throw' the players back into the narrative of the Hawks game, effectively saying: 'get yourselves out of that' (again).

In a similar way to the previous example, I recreated the precise time and score (82–70, 4:21) on the main scoreboard. I split the squad into two teams, one group being the five players on court in that moment. We then played a series of full-court 5-a-side games with two simple conditions: (1) each team is allowed one time-out, to be called by the players; and (2) the team behind scores double (e.g. 2-point shots are worth 4 – the idea was to recreate the Hawks' sense of momentum). The goal of the games, of course, was to win from the leading position, though I encouraged the players to use their timeouts to discuss ways of disrupting the defence within our offensive system. The losing team

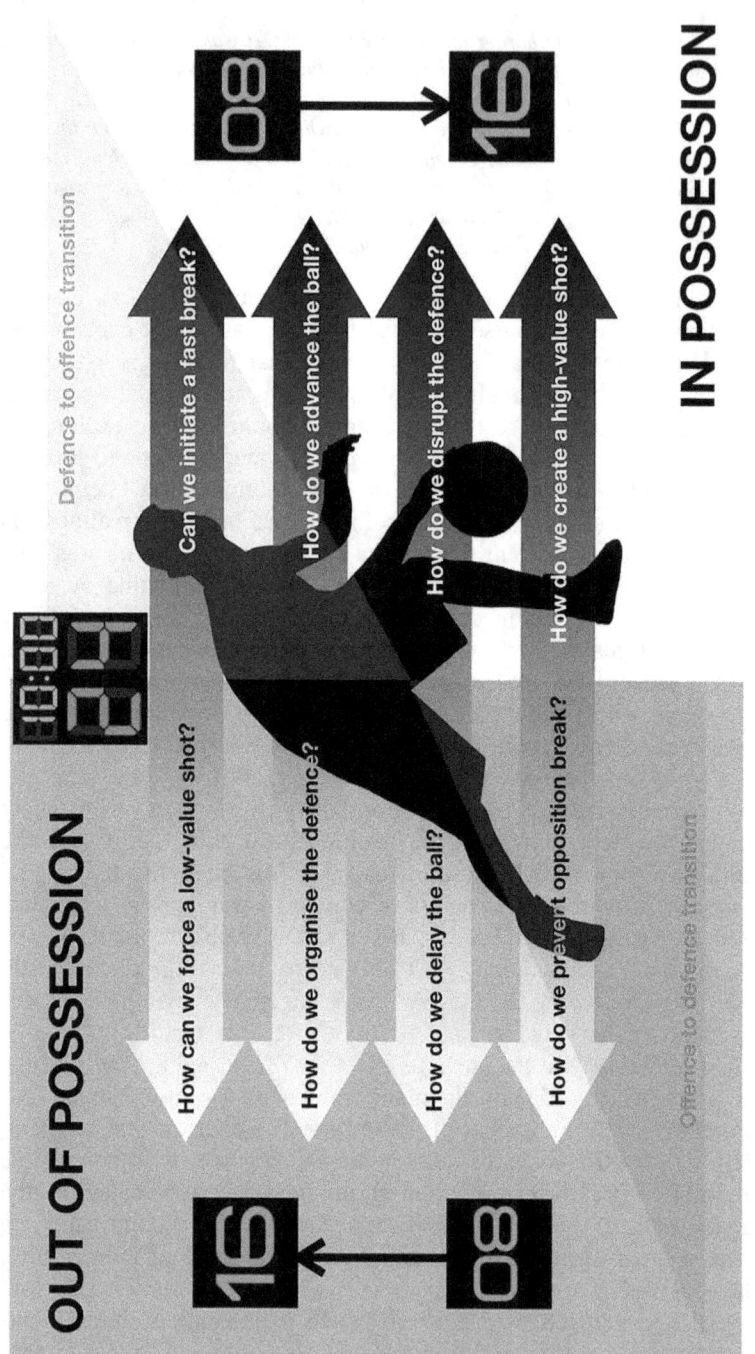

Figure 5.2 A game model of basketball.

in each game got a chance to shoot free-throws (i.e. make 7 out of 10) to avoid a running punishment. After each game I explored with the players how they *felt*; how this was similar (or not) to the Hawks game; what impact this had on their play, and what kinds of things we could do differently, in terms of self-talk, team talk and the offensive strategy. I wanted to help them recognise these emotions and to take more control of the situation into which they were 'thrown'.

Concluding remarks

Coupled with the previous conceptual chapter, we hope that these examples provide sufficient illustration for coaches to go and try the IGN approach. Whilst we have spent many years studying the theories and philosophical principles underpinning this approach, we argue that this is not necessary to begin to apply IGNs in any sporting context. As the two examples in this chapter illustrate, we believe that IGNs can be applied in *any* sport, with participants at *any* age or stage of development, and at *any* competitive level. Indeed, it is surely the drama, uncertainty, absurdity, anxiety, joy, relief and despair that sporting contests evoke that inspire us *all* to play (and coach). The IGN approach reminds us coaches to keep this simple idea front and centre.

References

Almond, L. (1986). Primary and secondary rules in games. In R. Thorpe, D. Bunker & L. Almond (eds), *Rethinking games teaching* (pp. 73–74). Loughborough: Loughborough University.

Bruner, J. (1960). *The process of education*. Cambridge, MA: Harvard University Press.

Bruner, J. (1966). *Toward a theory of instruction*. Cambridge, MA: Harvard University Press.

Harvey, S., Pill, S. & Almond, L. (2018). Old wine in new bottles: a response to claims that teaching games for understanding was not developed as a theoretically based pedagogical framework. *Physical Education and Sport Pedagogy*, 23(2), 166–180.

Headrick, J., Renshaw, I., Davids, K., Pinder, I. & Araujo, D. (2016). The dynamics of expertise acquisition in sport: the role of affective learning design. *Psychology of Sport and Exercise*, 16, 83–90.

Mitchell, S., Oslin, J. & Griffin, L. (2013). *Teaching sports concepts and skills: A tactical games approach*. Champaign, IL: Human Kinetics.

Serra-Olivares, J., Garcia-Lopez, L. & Calderon, A. (2016). Games-based approaches, pedagogical principles and tactical constraints: Examining games modification. *Journal of Teaching in Physical Education*, 35(3), 208–219.

Suits, B. (1978). *The grasshopper*. Ontario, CA: Broadview.

Tee, J., Ashford, M. & Piggott, D. (2018). A tactical periodization approach for rugby union. *Strength and Conditioning Journal*, 40(5), 1–13.

6 Skilfulness on country

Informal games and sports exposure

John Robert Evans, Richard Light and Greg Downey

This chapter reports on a 3-year Australian Research Council (ARC) study which examined the pedagogical influences on elite Indigenous players in the Australian Football League (AFL) and the National Rugby League (NRL). Indigenous athletes currently account for 14% of the elite player population in the AFL and NRL and this success far exceeds that of any other cultural group (Light & Evans 2018). Despite significant social disadvantage and alarming underachievement in many social determinants of health Indigenous Australians achieve remarkable success across a range of high profile male sports (Marmot, 2011).

Indigenous Australians' achievement in sport is often explained as a result of inherited, racial characteristics but, when seen as the result of a process of community culture and pedagogical influences, it demands inquiry into how this learning occurs and what socio-cultural factors facilitate it. The current academic discourse around learning has predominantly focused on a tight application of pedagogy. When pedagogy is viewed from a broader position it can be used to explain the success of Indigenous athletes in elite sport. In this case, the chapter identifies how the socio-cultural factors aligned with pedagogical factors that encourage and enhance achieving excellence at the highest levels of sport as a process of learning. In contemporary discussions about athlete centred pedagogy the environment for learning is often limited to the conditions that frame the regular episodes of training that occur as part of a regular season. However, this chapter broadens the scope of the environment to include the communities that indigenous athletes come from. In doing so it pays respect to the place of sport in many Indigenous communities (Gorman, 2012). The results in this chapter are based on a 3-year study funded by the ARC to examine the pedagogical factors enabling success in elite level team sport for Indigenous Australians.

Methodology

The study drew on both grounded theory and narrative enquiry to understand the data. The interpretive approach allowed for a deeper understanding of the participants' backgrounds in sport (Charmaz, 2006). The use of storytelling and the collection of life histories using oral accounts privileged Indigenous epistemologies such as storytelling (Archibald, Lee-Morgan & Santolo, 2019). The study sought to develop an understanding of the participants' experiences in sociocultural settings and how patterns of development and early life experience may have shaped the forms of expertise and skilfulness that Indigenous players bring to rugby league and Australian football (Light & Evans, 2017). The study also employed an Indigenous approach known as Dadirri to ensure the voice of the participants and their stories was captured (West, Stewart, Foster & Usher, 2012). Recruiting of the AFL participants involved an initial introduction from the AFL Players Association, and the cohort reflected a snowball sampling approach (Henry, 1990). The initial four NRL participants interviewed were known to the first author and the remaining four resulted from a snowball sampling approach. The sixteen participants in the study had well-established professional careers in the AFL and NRL. The data were collected using an initial life history interview with a minimum of questions except where clarification was required to establish critical milestones in participants' development. The analysis of the data identified a number of emerging theories across the participant pool, which were further developed in follow-up rounds of semi-structured interviews. Three interrelated factors which led to the development of expertise and skilfulness. These are discussed separately and included. Pseudonyms have been adopted to provide participant anonymity.

Results

Country, community and culture

The majority of participants in the study grew up in communities with easy access to open environments and natural settings (Dalton, Wilson, Evans & Cochrane, 2015). They used the term 'country' both to describe their cultural association and connection to a geographical area. Participants discussed how this environment contributed to learning to play sport. Carson, for example, made the following observation about how he felt being 'on country' and how this contributed to his development, including in sport:

Oh, but it is definitely different in country, like in rural places because you don't have that distraction. You don't have as many distractions as the city life, so you can, I don't know, you can express yourself in country and being close to country.

(Carson, Interview 1)

In these community situations, participants were immersed at early age in sport more generally, but also specifically in rugby league and Australian football. The cultural importance of sport in these community settings facilitates the early transfer and uptake of a sports culture related to participation and future excellence. This movement which starts on the periphery and moves towards greater participation over time appears seamless when Jamal explains: 'To be honest, I can't give you an exact day when I first kicked the footy, but from the stories from my mum as a pretty much a two-year-old, I was just obsessed with footy.' Rather than a structured introduction later in childhood through organised sport, participants in this study described an environment in which sport was more pervasive and encountered earlier in development. The participants were also able to develop their skills and participate in close-knit social and athletic communities where they could play with siblings and extended family. Jamal felt that he learnt about Australian football from playing with older brothers:

I obviously picked up the skills pretty quickly, and obviously having two older brothers, that's all we did in the front yard. And cousins as well. And just go down to the river on the grass just doing markers up and kicking and sort of honing the skills if you like.

(Jamal, Interview 1)

Their early experience was framed by community and family and associated with social life. This early experience was also not associated with sports clubs or explicit coaching. Participants in our study shared a strong feeling that playing sport was an expression of their distinctive culture and that this character was especially embodied in team sports rather than individual pursuits (Light & Evans, 2018). Earl's early exposure and enjoyment of rugby league is characterised by a strong cultural leaning towards team sports. He made the following observation of his engagement:

It's part of our culture to do things as a group, to enjoy each other's company and all that sort of stuff... Indigenous people play football the way they do and why they enjoy training the way they do.

(Earl, Interview 1)

The sociocultural environment which included immediate family, relatives and community members created a shared context that encouraged passionate engagement with Australian football and rugby league; these social conditions valued participation in football at a very early age and was a form of belonging. It contributed to sport being a dominant cultural practice. This shared community passion was also reflected in the support participants received in their trajectory to a professional career. Alex identified his father and uncles as football role models whose influence could he be heard when he commented on his exposure to Australian football and how this developed into a strong focus for his endeavours. Furthermore, his desire to fulfil his mother's hopes and a strong connection to his local community both made Alex want to be the best he could to make his family and community proud:

> Well my mum, like I said, that's the thing that sort of stuck in my mind, is that I wanted to make my family proud, like the people up in Darwin, make a name for myself. But also the big drive thing was to make her proud and pretty much say thank you in a way because you can never thank your parents enough.
>
> (Alex, Interview 1)

All of these factors suggest that sport was more thoroughly integrated into social and communal life than it is in many urban Australian communities. The early exposure, comprehensive social involvement, and enhanced motivation for excellence provided by this environment helps us to understand to some degree that the over-representation of Indigenous athletes at the most elite levels is likely linked to the importance of sport in their communities.

Exposure to a range of sports and games

Research suggests that early exposure to a range of different sports experience contributes toward enjoyment, continued participation and the development of expertise (Côté, 2005). Participants in this study were exposed to a range of sport and games growing up. This included, but was not limited to: boxing, cricket, athletics, basketball and rugby league to name a few. The players in this study did not simply participate in other sports; they also excelled and were elite performers in other sports and could have elected to pursue alternative athletic careers. For example, Max, who grew up in Darwin, on advice from his aunty, took up an offer of a rugby scholarship to an elite independent school in Sydney; only later would he shift his specialty to Australian football. Playing sports other than football was also a part of community life, and a diverse range of sports were commonly played at family and community gatherings:

> The earliest memory of growing up was pretty much going to parties, going to barbeques, cousins, uncles, and it would be always sport. Whether it was the game we used to play, fly, or we'd play other games, ball games, soccer. Cricket was a big thing. We'd always have two teams, and cricket would go all day, just in the backyard. So it was a thirty-by-thirty metre perimeter, and we'd play cricket morning 'til sunset and, yeah, a lot of it was around sport.
>
> (Nathaniel, Interview 1)

Although some of the literature focuses on the role of specialisation in the emergence of expertise, the social context of skill development in these communities encouraged diverse, highly engaged practice as a pervasive part of social life. Max who had not played Australian football before the age of 10 credited his exposure to other game forms, such as playing association football (soccer) and basketball, helped him make the transition. His first exposure to Australian football was through participating in backyard game forms learnt from new friends and at school. He subsequently joined a local club and claimed that he was able to learn quickly due to his basketball experience. Max elaborated on this when he said:

> Playing basketball at school, playing just at club level, had a massive influence to actually working out angles, to be able to bounce the ball and look up and do three things at once. You've got to bounce the ball. You've got to look at where your team mates are, so it actually made you multitask altogether, and I think the beautiful thing about football is that if you're carrying the ball in your hand, you don't have to bounce it, so there's only one thing to think about, how you're going to execute that ball.
>
> (Max, Interview 1)

If anything, Max's account suggested that the tasks he confronted in Australian football were actually less complicated perceptual and coordination feats than those he performed in other sports. Max gained important tactical understanding in Australian football and particularly through the modified games that he created and played with friends. Jarrod 'grew up playing soccer and little athletics' and engaged in footy at school where he also participated in cricket and enjoyed all sports. He moved to Darwin at age 10 and took up rugby league: 'I always played rugby when I got to Darwin. I was a sort of rugby man.' But he also continued playing footy and cricket at school. Nathaniel captures the central role sport occupied in the lives of the participants in this study as they grew up as well as the range of sports they enjoyed:

> I think growing up and playing a lot of sport… I think it helped develop my hand-eye coordination and my probably aerobic capacity. In high school, I wasn't physically as strong as everybody else, but I knew I had the skills, you know, the skills to play the game. So the things I was doing without even knowing were helping me become a football player. Doing it just out of the love of playing touch football at lunchtime or you know, playing soccer on the footy field, just yeah, it put me in the position that I am today.
> (Nathaniel, Interview 1)

In this account, we see, not just the role of deliberate play for generating the motivation and sustained practice necessary for elite expertise to emerge, but also the way that diversity in sporting experience created a kind of naïve cross-training to encourage a wide variety of skills and physical capacities to grow.

Learning through informal and modified games

Informal games had a major impact on learning during the early years of participation in sport for all the participants in the study. Chances to play with other members in the community, taking into account the diversity of constraints and opportunities, were important developmental activities. Participation in informal games was also a reflection of the sociocultural environments which were experienced by the participants, including the absence of formally organised sporting activities.

The participants' interview responses, correspondingly, did not place a heavy emphasis on the role of coaches and participation in organised sport but rather singled out informal games as the greatest influence on their emerging ability to play rugby league and Australian football (AFL) in their early years. Whereas youth coaches, including professional or semi-professional experts who play a gate-keeping role for elite opportunities and selection to representative teams, may play a key role in youth development in urban sport, they were virtually absent from our participants' accounts of their sporting biographies. Alex, for example, suggested the value of informal games and the fact that they often 'don't get noticed' as well as their implicit nature. The participants, instead of engaging in structured play, would rather emulate their NRL and AFL heroes by replicating their movements and plays in backyard games, sometimes by experimenting and innovating with materials that were readily available in the environment. Exposure from a young age, especially in regional and rural areas, to play, often against siblings, cousins and extended family, provided opportunities to solve problems in an environment which encouraged experimentation. The participants designed informal games or ran staged patterns of interaction with the local constraints taken into account. Alex goes on to make this observation about play with friends and siblings in his early years:

> [We used to kick] anything shaped like a football, that's how bad we were. This [plastic] bottle – its shape [indicating an object found nearby] – so we used to kick around two-litre Coke bottles. There was always a special ... the ways to make it a lot more harder, so it's better to kick. But we just had to be aware, I guess, of hitting the wrong tip of the bottle. But we kicked toilet rolls, stubby coasters in the house, put goals everywhere in the yards, and that's just how it was.
>
> (Alex, Interview 1)

Alex's reflections also indicate how creativity was fostered by the need to adapt to local conditions and lack of resources. This necessity for innovation was a feature discussed by all the participants in that they organised games to suit the available equipment, playing surfaces, and numbers of players. Again, this contrasts with models of how elite skills should be nurtured in organised, urban sport in that these activities are often seen to demand infrastructure investment, high quality facilities, and the provision of official equipment. The model from the Indigenous community, in contrast, suggests that innovation and the capacity to participate in sport at a high level might be facilitated by greater situated variation and creative problem solving within the activity setting. This is further enhanced when Jamal discusses how playing games designed with friends refined his skills, in this case a game they improvised on a basketball court called 'court footy':

> That's where you learn that sort of backyard skills. It just becomes natural. It just all happens, and you don't think about it because

you're playing with your mates, playing with your cousins. You just enjoying it and is not really structured. It's just, have fun, enjoy yourself and whether that was in my court, whether it was in my mate's court against his brothers. There was a group of six against six or seven of them.

(Jamal, Interview 1)

In his discussion about the role of informal games and other sports, Max was adamant about their place in his development:

I think [their influence was] massive, especially like with soccer and stuff in Downton (Northern Territory) because I have a lot of cousins around me. We were always doing stuff down at the place called the low level, and we'd all have barbies and that, and that was it. That's where you learned all your skills, you know. You'd chase your older cousins around and that sort of stuff. So I think that was massive in the ... obviously, the early development.

(Max, interview 1)

Rather than access to highly structured and formal opportunities, these accounts point to the role of informality and variation the game setting for encouraging robust skill development.

Discussion

Indigenous NRL and AFL players have been recognised for their exceptional skilfulness (Gorman, 2012; Hallinan & Judd, 2009). However as noted by Gorman there was no 'recognition of the hours of training and application they [the Indigenous athletes] put in' (Gorman, 2011, p. 8), especially within the unique settings that framed this practice. Their skilfulness emerged from community based often informal in nature but deeply embedded in local culture.

Hours spent in distinctive forms of play, their exposure to other game forms and informal games likely contributes, not just to a heightened level of skilfulness, but also to the distinctive types of skill that Indigenous athletes bring to the AFL. For example, the fact that informal play environments necessarily demand creativity, improvisation, and innovation makes it easy to see how the widely acknowledged 'creativity' of elite Indigenous athletes emerges as the outgrowth of informal training regimes that are ideal for cultivating the trait.

The participants in this study demonstrate the importance of the socio-cultural (community) context in learning to play Australian football, as in any sport (Coyle, 2009). The influences experienced in the early years of development are expressed in adulthood as exceptional skills. While non-Indigenous peers may experience similar conditions, we argue that they are more central to the development of many Indigenous players, reinforced by social life and even cultural identity. The early immersion of Indigenous players in sport is a highly valued part of community life. Their expertise is rooted in a broader process of socialisation where learning was implicit and arose naturally from forms of social interaction. This early entry into sport as a facet of socialisation aligns with Bourdieu's views about implicit pedagogy and evidence in the work of Wacquant (1995), who argued that this informal training resulted in a particular habitus. Lave and Wenger's (1991) theory of situated learning also provides a way of discussing the early informal and unstructured apprenticeships that Indigenous players experience in communities of practice; they entered sports at the periphery at an early age and, as their capacities grew, moved towards a deeper engagement over time. Participation in sport was taken up as an embedded cultural and social practice, rather than as a special purpose activity confined to formal settings. The connection of sporting excellence to everyday culture and 'country', even in its most traditional forms, can be seen in Gorman's book where Michael Long describes how hunting on his traditional grounds contributed to his ability to be effective and provide sure footed certainty in playing days. Over and over, Indigenous athletes describe their sporting excellence as emerging from the pervasive activities of daily life, not from specialised settings in which excellence itself was ever a goal.

The Indigenous athletes' stories of attaining a level of skilfulness which translates into being an expert or exceptional performer shows the requirement for practice over time. Our research suggests that the composition of those hours benefits if the contexts are structured in a variety of ways: that is, optimum learning contexts may be constructed in diverse ways. Among the participants' accounts from this study, organised practice did not appear as a prominent element or theme in the development of their expertise. Early specialisation, while evident in some cases, was also accompanied by exposure to other game forms, such as informal and improvised games, as well as to other sports.

Conclusion

The experience of these elite athletes demonstrates how important a variety of developmental activities are, not only for maintaining motivation of young athletes, but also for the cultivation of sophisticated traits such as creativity, rapid problem solving, innovation, and the capacity to improvise in unstructured play. The accounts provide insight for coaches and researchers alike into the value of game-based approaches as forms of 'training' that are more spontaneous and driven by the participants themselves.

References

Archibald, J.-A., Lee-Morgan, J. & Santolo, J. D. (Eds.). (2019). *Decolonizing research: Indigenous storywork as methodology*. Chicago, IL: Zed Books.

Charmaz, K. (2006). *Constructing grounded theory: a practical guide through qualitative analysis*. London: Sage.

Côté, J. (2005). *Sport expertise in the lives of children and adolescents*. Paper presented at the Applied Sport Expertise and Learning Workshop, Canberra.

Coyle, D. (2009). *The talent code*. New York: Random House.

Dalton, B., Wilson, R., Evans, J. R. & Cochrane, S. (2015). Australian Indigenous youth's participation in sport and associated health outcomes: Empirical analysis and implications. *Sport Management Review*, 18(1), 57–68.

Gorman, S. (2011). *Legends: the AFL Indigenous Team of the Century*. Acton, ACT: Aboriginal Studies Press.

Gorman, S. (2012). Voices from the boundary line: the Australian Football League's Indigenous Team of the Century. *Sport in Society*, 15(7), 1014–1025.

Hallinan, C. & Judd, B. (2009). Changes in assumptions about Australian Indigenous Footballers: From exclusion to enlightenment. *The International Journal of the History of Sport*, 26(16), 2358–2375.

Henry, G. T. (1990). *Practical sampling*. Newbury Park, CA: Sage.

Lave, J. & Wenger, E. (1991). *Situated learning legitimate peripheral participation*. Cambridge: Cambridge University Press.

Light, R. L. & Evans, J. R. (2017). Socialisation, culture and the foundations of expertise in elite level Indigenous Australian sportsmen. *Sport, Education and Society*, 22(7), 852–863.

Light, R. L. & Evans, J. R. (2018). *Indigenous stories of success in Australian sport: Journeys to the AFL and NRL*. London: Palgrave Macmillan.

Marmot, M. (2011). Social determinants and the health of Indigenous Australians. *Medical Journal of Australia*, 194(10), 512–513.

Wacquant, L. J. D. (1995). Pugilistic point of view: How boxers think and feel about their trade. *Theory and Society*, 24(4), 489–535.

West, R., Stewart, L., Foster, K. & Usher, K. (2012). Through a critical lens: Indigenist research and the Dadirri method. *Qualitative Health Research*, 22(11), 1582–1590.

7 Sport in physical education
Evidencing learning from employing a game-based approach in badminton

Stephen Harvey and Matthew Pomeroy

In this chapter, we outline how we collaborated on designing a five-day badminton unit for which student learning data were collected. The game-based approach (GBA) adopted in this project was Teaching Games for Understanding (TGfU: Bunker & Thorpe, 1982). Matt reflects on the results he drew from his data collection and we offer suggestions on how teachers and sport coaches may go about a similar process to Matt in their own local contexts.

Background

Matt

In the beginning of his career, Matt used mainly direct instruction and kept skills and strategies isolated from each other. Matt followed many of the lessons from a co-teacher. After joining Twitter about ten years ago, Matt began to see that there were other models of instruction that were very useful and effective as alternatives to direct instruction. Matt learned more about a GBA for sport teaching in PE. He became very passionate about a GBA, probably because he observed that students were challenged mentally and physically, and he could tell that students enjoyed learning that way.

At this same time, Stephen had begun to share more information about GBA on social media and Matt thought this would be a great time to change up how he was teaching his badminton units. Matt had begun to add some modified games that incorporated skills and strategies to his units already but was ready to formally embrace a GBA.

Stephen

Stephen and Matt formally met when Matt was Stephen's moderator for his 2016 Physedagogy PhysEdSummit Session on Questioning in a

GBA. At this time, in his role as a university Professor, Stephen had begun a period of working collaboratively with teachers using collaborative action research (CAR[1]) to gather data to create 'stories' or narratives on the efficacy of GBAs in 'real-world' settings for a presentation at the 2017 Society for Health and Physical Educators (SHAPE) of America convention in Boston. Ultimately, the process of identifying an area of need and working collaboratively with an expert 'sport pedagogue' in that domain can help drive improvements in teachers' practice. Consequently, Matt and Stephen began to collaborate on a badminton unit in preparation for the conference, which is the focus of this chapter.

Local context and overview of the game-based badminton unit

Matt teaches 7th and 8th grade classes at Merton Intermediate School and gets to see his students every day in quarters 1 and 4 for PE class. During the 2nd and 3rd quarters, where this badminton unit was placed, he alternates between Health and PE class. In these quarters most of the classes are indoors due to weather and the various teachers rotate into and out of the gym and other spaces available to them around the school. This means the faculty run five-day units for these quarters. That said, students are taught badminton every year from 5th grade.

Matt taught this badminton unit to 224 7th and 8th grade students separated across eight different classes. Matt met each class for 41-minutes every other day for two weeks, and a total of six class periods. Class size ranged from 24–30 students. Classes met in a gymnasium which housed six full-sized badminton courts, and two half courts on one side of the gym. Thus, there was enough room for each student to play on one-half court, so no-one had to sit out.

In terms of planning and delivery of the unit, Matt suggested that he start with a game form on day 1 of the unit where students played tournament games. The notion was that the initial 1 versus 1 half-court games would build students game appreciation on day 1, which is the first and, arguably, the most important aspect of the TGfU model. Participating in skills drills and additional modified/conditioned game forms on days 2 and 3 then provided the necessary foundational skills (i.e. drop shots, clear, smash, etc.) to return back to game play on days 4, 5 and 6. Matt noted to Stephen at the outset that he may not be able to follow a typical TGfU game-skill practice-game cycle in a lesson, so Stephen suggested the Clinic Game-Day format for this unit where games are played on one day, and developed skills during skill clinics the next day, followed by another games day (Alexander & Penney, 2005).

Table 7.1 Badminton middle school block plan outline using a Clinic Game-Day Model.

Day	Content
1	Team Sport Assessment Procedure (TSAP: Grehaigne, Richard & Griffin, 2005) Tournament Games for pre-assessment
2	Tactical problem: Hitting to and defending space on the court • On the shuttle skills: Serving, clears and slow drops • Off the shuttle skills: movement back and front
3	Tactical problem: Winning and preventing point scoring • On the shuttle skills: Fast drop and smashes, blocks • Off the shuttle skills: movement back and front and side to side
4	Singles tournament play – using a ladder format • See-saw assessment
5	Singles tournament play – using a ladder format • See-saw assessment
6	Tournament Games for TSAP post assessment

SHAPE America Grade level outcomes (GLOs; 2013):
- Creates open space in net-wall games with either a long- or short-handled implement by varying force or direction or by moving opponent from side to side and/or forward and back. (S2.M7.8)
- Varies placement, force, and timing of return to prevent anticipation by the opponent. (S2.M8.8)
- Demonstrates the mature form of forehand and backhand strokes with a short- or long-handled implement with power and accuracy in net games such as pickleball, tennis, badminton or paddle ball. (S1.M14.8)
- Executes consistently (at least 70% of the time) a legal underhand serve for distance and accuracy for net-wall games such as badminton, volleyball or pickleball. (S1.M12.8)

Assessing student learning

Hay (2006) argued that assessment has two central purposes – accountability *and* learning – suggesting a shift from assessment *of* learning to assessment *for* learning. Assessment *of* learning is generally associated with end-of-unit summative assessments while assessment *for* learning is *ongoing* assessment, which recognises the need to inform and provide feedback to students on their progress so as to modify their learning *within* the tasks they are engaged in during a unit of work. Hay (2006) also noted that an assessment *for* learning perspective calls for using authentic assessment tasks and go hand in hand with their instructional function. In an attempt to an attempt to align curriculum, instruction, and assessment and ensure that the students were being assessed within the context in which the skills are being developed (i.e. *in* the game),

Stephen suggested Matt use TSAP (Grehaigne et al., 2005) to assess student learning in the psychomotor domain. Matt felt that the TSAP would be a great way to see the degree to which each of the students in his classes attained the GLOs specified at the outset of the unit (see Table 7.1), and a further benefit was that the students were involved in the assessment process. Thus, not only did the students assist in generating valuable data by administering the assessment, through peer observing and assessing, they also saw examples of what successful skills and strategies looked like, which would help stimulate discussion for the rest of the unit. Indeed, the TSAP was developed had the notion of peer assessment in mind when it was constructed, and thus was based on a constructivist learning theory (Grehaigne et al., 2005).

While there is limited published research on the use of the TSAP in net-wall games, previous research on player/student use of the TSAP in invasion games has shown that in less than an hour of observation training, learners were able to assess performance with a moderate level of reliability, which may be a sufficient level of reliability for practicing teachers to be able to use it for formative assessment purposes like we are showcasing this current chapter (Nadeau, Godbout & Richard, 2008). Moreover, the constant iterations between game play and reflection supported by statistics generated by observers using the TSAP analyses enables performers to bring aspects of the game forward for interpretation and reflection. This enables learners to debate and then, through additional game play, test and validate the most appropriate solutions.

For the cognitive domain, while Stephen initially provided Matt with some declarative and procedural knowledge content questions drawn from McGee and Farrow (1987) and Matt intended to put these on a Google quiz to help him collect the data, Matt independently decided to design his own, more authentic cognitive domain assessment, a pre-post-unit SeeSaw^2 assessment. To assess student development in the affective domain, Stephen suggested Matt have his students complete the Intrinsic Motivation Inventory (perceived competence, interest/enjoyment, and effort/importance scales: Ryan, 1982). The rationale behind this was understanding how the students were feeling about the unit and the activities, Matt would be able to explore these feelings with the students through asking pertinent questions and make any necessary adjustments to the unit where needed.

Team sport assessment procedure

On day 1, Matt had agreed with Stephen that it was imperative students got involved playing small-sided (i.e., on one half of a full badminton court) 1 versus 1 games. To do this, Matt set up various mini tournaments of 4–5 players. Matt printed tournament sheets and located at each court. Since this structure was already in place, Matt built the TSAP data collection into this structure by printing enough TSAP forms for each individual student at each court. Before the games started, Matt quickly covered the game form rules and outlined what the peer observers were assessing on the TSAP form and who was completing which assessment on who. By planning this out, this same tournament and procedure was then intact for the final day of the unit, thus, giving Matt reliable and valid data on the degree to which each of the students in his classes attained the GLOs specified at the outset of the unit.

At the end of all day 1 classes, Matt had three games worth of data on his students. Matt designed a Google form that the student could use to plug their numbers into and submit. With the students doing data entry, assessment information was compiled in less than five minutes of class time. With the data inputted Matt then accessed the Google sheet linked to the initial Google form and computed efficiency index and performance scores for each student using the formulas below:

- Efficiency index is (volley / 2 + successful shots) / (10 + lost ball)
- Performance score is calculated by (received ball / 2) + (efficiency index × 10)^3

Cognitive domain

Using the SeeSaw assessment created another opportunity for the students to showcase what they had learned. On day 1, the students each gathered minute of footage of them playing during a singles match. The students were required to watch their video and reflect on the different shots they used, and to see how much they moved their opponent around the court. On day 5 of the unit, students then 'played out' a perfect game situation as if they could perform any shot. The thought was that Matt would be able to hear the student verbalise their developments in knowledge that they accumulated over the course of the unit, even if they couldn't successfully perform the skill. This procedure is much like the Verbal Protocol Analysis Procedure used in-between points in tennis (McPherson, 2008), which gives insights into the tactical knowledge development of the students over time. Matt later found out that Stephen has used something where he had players observe each other, but rather than assessing game performance like in the TSAP, students had to act like a sports commentator and verbalise the action. In a soccer-focused study Stephen showed students improved the sophistication of the tactical knowledge over a 11–13-lesson unit of soccer (Harvey, Gil-Arias & Claver, 2020). Units of similar length to Matt's, however, did show improvement when used by research in badminton with similar aged students to those in Matt's classes (French, Werner, Rink, Taylor & Hussey, 1996; French, Werner, Taylor, Hussey & Jones, 1996).

Affective domain

The final piece of data that Stephen helped Matt implement was the affective domain survey. This survey was administered to all of Matt's 7th and 8th grade students in the beginning part of the badminton unit. The intrinsic motivation questions were focused on net-wall units (including the current badminton unit) units that Matt was going to teach over the next month or two of school. The questions were rated on a 1–7 Likert scale (1 = not true at all, 7 = very true; see Table 7.2).

Table 7.2 IMI questions.

Affective concept	Questions
Perceived competence	I think I am pretty good at this activity.
	I think I did pretty well at this activity, compared to other students.
	After working at this activity for a while, I felt pretty competent.
	I am satisfied with my performance at this task.
	I was pretty skilled at this activity.
	This was an activity that I could not do very well. (Reverse Scored Item; R)
Interest/enjoyment	I enjoyed doing this activity very much
	This activity was fun to do.
	I thought this was a boring activity. (R)
	This activity did not hold my attention at all. (R)
	I would describe this activity as very interesting.
	I thought this activity was quite enjoyable.
	While I was doing this activity, I was thinking about how much I enjoyed it.
Effort/importance	I put a lot of effort into this.
	I did not try very hard to do well at this activity. (R)
	I tried very hard on this activity.
	It was important to me to do well at this task.
	I did not put much energy into this. (R)

Reflection

What happened?

Below are the results (based on 185 of the 224 students) of the TSAP. The results showed that the badminton unit worked in terms of developing the students' psychomotor skills.

Although Matt did not use a rubric or coding procedures from French and colleagues' two studies (1996) to assess the students verbalisations from the authentic SeeSaw assessment, anecdotally, Matt noticed that students were definitely able to talk to each other in more sophisticated ways about their game play performance.

In terms of the affective domain[4], the results showed that when asked to rate their competence (i.e. skill level at badminton), 65% of students had a positive viewpoint of their skill level. In terms of their enjoyment, 75% of students thought net-wall activities were fun, which meant the vast majority of students enjoyed the unit. Similarly, the majority of students (60%) thought that it was important to do well in these activities, but it was interesting that 25% didn't think it was that important. When asked their thoughts on whether net-wall games held their attention, approximately 72% of students thought they did. Another positive was that 74% of students responded that they would try hard in net-wall games. However, these results did reveal that while the majority of class had positive views about their competence and enjoyment of net-wall games, there was approximately 25% who viewed net-wall sports, and their competence in these sports, less favourably. However, due to the lack of pre-post survey data, we are unable to state whether the current unit changed any of these students' perceptions of their competence.

As well as the data Matt generated, Stephen asked Matt to identify 'three stars and a wish' from his badminton unit. Matt identified:

Three stars:

- Lots of activity including opportunities to respond (i.e. birdies hit) though small-sided 1 versus 1 rallies and singles games. On average,

Table 7.3 Pre-post test team sport assessment procedure scores

	Pre-test average	Post-test average	% Gain
Efficiency index	1.35	2.08	54%
Performance score	20.1	52.73	101%

82% (27/33 minutes) of class was dedicated to active lessons. This is what potentially gave such good post-test TSAP scores.
- Development of skills/strategies together in a game situation – When organising the games and activities, there was always a focus on a specific skill. When skills are taught through the game or after playing a game with the game context in mind, Matt found that students were excited to use the skills they were learning and were more engaged in the activity. This was shown in the affective domain results.
- Ongoing formative assessments (i.e. on 4/6 days) that helped feedback to students that informed them about their progress and learning. The interaction between playing time and analysing others led to high levels of learning.

One wish:

- If it was possible, Matt would have liked to extend this unit to a 7–8 day unit, because it could allow for more skill development work and tactical/strategy practice. Matt could also extend the singles games into using more modified/conditioned 1 versus 1 games, some full-court singles games, and help build in some doubles play.

So what?

One of the things Matt likes about a GBA is how the games are organised into game categories, which provides the teacher with the ability to leverage the transfer of knowledge from one game to another (see Mitchell, Oslin & Griffin, 2013). This notion of transfer is especially important when Matt is constrained into only having five-day units on one activity area. Moving forward, when Matt teaches his other net-wall games like nitroball, eclipse ball, sepak takraw, pickleball, volleyball, table ball, and tennis he will now have the ability to leverage the knowledge students gained in this specific badminton unit. Indeed, while Matt acknowledges that some of the technical skill requirements are different in other net-wall games, for the next academic year, Matt suggested it might be possible to put several net-wall units into quarters 2 and 3 of his school year to take advantage of transfer.

While the TSAP provided Matt with valuable information on the psychomotor developments in his students against the GLOs, Matt did feel that TSAP assessments were somewhat rushed for a 40-minute class. The first TSAP assessment felt the most rushed, because the students quickly needed to learn the rules, how to measure the assessment, and then play up to four short games. The final TSAP assessment didn't seem as rushed, because they had been participating in badminton activities for the previous five days and they had already used the assessment.

Conclusions

Given that sport teaching in physical education and sport coaching share a common concern with player technical and tactical game development the TSAP can be used to validate what we are doing as physical education and sport practitioners, especially to our organisational administrators. Moreover, and similar to Harvey and Gittins's use of video review in the context of a game-based soccer unit (Harvey & Gittins, 2014), the SeeSaw assessment gave students the opportunity to showcase their learning, which could be an additional tool for physical educators and sport coaches as an assessment 'as' and/or 'for' learning tool, especially when resources are limited. Reading this chapter demonstrates how elements of GBA developed for sport coaching, such as the TSAP, can be used in sport teaching in PE.

Notes

1 As an extension of Action Research, CAR helps stimulate the development of new knowledge and understandings for practitioners by systematically and critically reflecting on their practice as its enacted in an ongoing manner.
2 SeeSaw is a digital platform assessment tool: https://web.seesaw.me/why-seesaw
3 Matt provides more information about his use of the TSAP on his blog – see www.pomeroyshpe.com/pomeroys-health–pe-blog/my-journey-to-implement-tsap-team-sports-assessment-procedure-a-tgfu-badminton-unit
4 Student responses to the affective domain survey questions were taken after the first two lessons of unit. Ideally, Matt would have generated pre-post unit data, but this was not possible due to logistical issues.

References

Alexander, K. & Penney, D. (2005). Teaching under the influence: Feeding Games for Understanding into the Sport Education development-refinement cycle. *Physical Education & Sport Pedagogy*, 10(3), 287–301.
Bunker, D. & Thorpe, R. (1982). A model for the teaching of games in secondary schools. *Bulletin of Physical Education*, 18(1), 5–8.
Evans, J. & Light, R. (2008). Coach development through collaborative action research: A rugby coach's implementation of game sense pedagogy. *Asian Journal of Exercise and Sport Science*, 5(1), 31–37.

French, K. E., Werner, P., Rink, J. E., Taylor, K. & Hussey, K. (1996). The effects of a 3-week unit of tactical, skill or combined tactical and skill instruction on badminton performance of ninth grade students. *Journal of Teaching in Physical Education*, 15(4), 418–438.

French, K. E., Werner, P., Taylor, K., Hussey, K. & Jones, J. (1996). The effects of a 6-week unit of tactical, skill or combined tactical and skill instruction of badminton performance of ninth grade students. *Journal of Teaching in Physical Education*, 15(4), 439–463.

Grehaigne, J. F., Richard, J. F. & Griffin, L. (2005). *Teaching and learning team sports and games*. New York: Routledge Falmer.

Harvey, S. & Gittins, C. (2014). Effects of integrating video-based feedback into a Teaching Games for Understanding soccer unit. *AGORA for Physical Education and Sport*, 16(3), 271–290.

Harvey, S., Gil-Arias, A. & Claver, F. (2020). Effects of Teaching Games for Understanding on tactical knowledge development in middle school physical education. *Journal of Physical Education and Sport*, 20(3), 1369–1379.

Hay, P. J. (2006). Assessment for learning in physical education. In D. Kirk, M. O'Sullivan & D. Macdonald (eds) *The handbook of physical education* (pp. 312–325). London: Sage.

McGee, R. & Farrow, A. (1987). *Test questions for physical education activities*. Champaign, IL: Human Kinetics.

McPherson, S. L. (2008). Tactics: using knowledge to enhance performance. In D. Farrow, J. Baker & C. MacMahon (eds), *Developing sport expertise: Researchers and coaches put theory into practice* (pp. 155–167). London: Routledge.

Mitchell, S., Oslin, J. & Griffin, L. (2013). *Teaching sport concepts and skills: A Tactical Games Approach for ages 7 to 18*. Champaign, IL: Human Kinetics.

Nadeau, L., Godbout, P. & Richard, J.-F. (2008). Assessment of ice hockey performance in real-game conditions. *European Journal of Sports Science*, 8 (6), 379–388.

Ryan, R. M. (1982). Control and information in the intrapersonal sphere: An extension of cognitive evaluation theory. *Journal of Personality and Social Psychology*, 43(3), 450–462.

SHAPE America. (2013). *Grade-level outcomes for K-12 physical education*. Reston, VA: Author.

8 Learning to be a game-changer

Adrian P. Turner

It's 3:00 p.m. on 9 July 2019, and a text message has just indicated that the coach, who oversees 'drop-in' soccer, will be unable to attend the event this evening. As the coaching facilitator, Jimmy Smith (pseudonym), will need to coordinate the event from 6:00 to 7:15 p.m. Drop-in soccer is a program that the local soccer club in a small town in the American Midwest offers twice a week throughout the summer months, at no financial cost, that encourages youth soccer players to learn to play the game in a city park. There are two small 2-metre goals, erected in the grass area and secured with goal anchors about 32 metres apart. Players range in ages from 8 to 14 and it is impossible to predict how many players will attend – numbers sometimes vary from 6 to 35 players. The temperature is 31°C at 5:45 p.m. and coach Jimmy has brought to the location: four pop-up soccer goals, player pinafores, marker domes and a variety of soccer balls.

At 6:00 p.m. there are four players present, a brother and sister (8- and 10-year-olds) and two older boys (11- and 12-year-olds). A car arrives and three additional players alight – another brother and sister (11- and 14-year-olds) and a 13-year-old boy who used to play with the club. Simultaneously, a 14-year-old boy arrives on his bicycle. Coach Jimmy knows most of the players – both the 14-year-old boys are skilful players on the club's oldest age-group team. The youngest siblings are very tenacious. Before they start to play Jimmy rapidly estimates the ability of the participants and nonchalantly hands blue pinafores to four of them to create teams that equate in terms of gender, age and playing ability. While the goals provide a frame of reference for the goal-lines there are no boundaries marked to designate the width of the field. The ground rises towards a tree on one side of the field, which serves as a natural boundary and the players observe a similar distance on the other side as out-of-bounds. The field is about 25 metres wide and players take throw-ins, goal-kicks and corners when the ball goes out of play. They select a size four soccer ball for their game. It's typically used by 9–12-year-olds but the older players are familiar with smaller futsal soccer balls from their indoor training in elementary school gymnasia in the winter.

The game begins with the stipulation that after every score both goalkeepers will switch positions with an outfield player. Goals are frequent but if play continues for longer than five minutes, without a goal, then both goalkeepers are changed – the coach observes the time. As the 4 versus 4 game develops over the initial minutes the goalkeeper becomes a crucial figure functioning as a sweeper-keeper, collecting over hit passes from opponents and then distributing the ball out of defence. The goalkeeper also provides an outlet for each team to provide depth in attack and recycle the ball when a team cannot play the ball forward due to defensive pressure forcing play away from the goal. At about 6:15 p.m. Jimmy pauses the game for a water-break. Another car arrives and two 11-year-old boys, accompanied by their parents, emerge. One additional player is assimilated into each team (now 5 versus 5) as play resumes at about 6:20 p.m. During the game, the ball is typically passed over short distances along the ground but the 13-year-old male player is quite skilful and constantly looking to play the ball longer in the air to his team's target player, one of the 14-year-old boys. Sometimes, this pass is over hit as the ball travels over the goal-line. The players self-referee their game – handball is only observed if it is deliberate or denies a goal. A penalty kick is awarded when a ball hits a defender's arm on his own goal line. The playing area is crowded and about to become increasingly congested as two additional players arrive on their bicycles around 6:35 p.m. They exclaim that they thought 'drop-ins' started at 6:30 p.m. One player is a 13-year-old boy and the other a 12-year-old girl. They join the respective teams creating a 6 versus 6 game.

Game play is halted after a few minutes to allow the players to get water and the teams provided an opportunity to discuss a question posed by the coach in their respective huddles. 'How will your team now set up to incorporate additional team members?' The players take a few minutes to discuss their solution and do not respond directly to the coach. Instead, it can be observed from their restart positions at kick-off that in addition to a goalkeeper, one team uses a formation with two defenders, two midfielders and a striker; the other team sets up with a goalkeeper, one defender, two midfielders and two attackers. After five minutes a timeout is called by the coach and a second question posed to both the teams respectively to discuss in team huddles. 'How can you still be successful now that game play has changed with four additional players on the same field (6 versus 6) compared to when the game started with 4 versus 4 teams?' After several minutes of discussion, one team's response is that they need to pass the ball more rapidly. The other team (with two defenders in their formation) suggests that from the goalkeeper the ball should be passed to either flank defender with a short pass because players are very congested in the centre of the small field. The coach asks, 'Will that always work in the game?' After discussion, the other team suggests that if the wide players are covered the goalkeeper could pass the ball into the middle instead or try a slightly longer pass into space behind the opposition defenders. The coach also inquires, 'What do you think about your revised game?' The players respond that while play is more chaotic they enjoy working with more players and would prefer to remain in the larger game which they perceive as requiring more skilful performance. The coach suggests that in addition to their newly described tactics both teams might consider utilising their goalkeepers as shot-stoppers only, rather than sweeper-keepers, as this will create more space in the playing area for the outfield players. It also provides an opportunity for players to rest when they are goalkeeping but still participate in the game during the humid conditions.

Despite the variety in ages and ability levels the players work well together in the session until this point. While play is competitive it is also quite respectful. Participants do not engage in a physical game that might exist in other soccer playing cultures. The two 14-year-old boys bring the other players into the game with their passing play, but as the coach continues to observe it is noticeable that some of the younger players are beginning to tire and the older players are starting to become more dominant, retaining possession of the ball, dribbling for longer time periods and beginning to score more frequently. They also are adopting more offensive positions on both teams. At 6:50 p.m. play is stopped for a penultimate water-break. The two boys who arrived with their parents indicate that they are tired but their parents coax them into continuing after a drink and the boys are both responsive. The coach decides to intervene during the final segment of play. Throughout the game both teams have gone on goal-scoring runs and although an official score has not been recorded, scoring has been fairly equal. Coach Jimmy announces that the game score is tied and everything will remain the same except for two players on each team. Anyone may still score, but a goal scored by either of these two team-nominated players will count double. The final game segment will last for 10 minutes, running clock. After a collective 'ooh' of excitement the teams immediately request a minute to discuss their revised game strategy.

Both teams select a combination of younger/less skilled players as their nominated goal-scorers. When play resumes, it is evident that teams have moved their nominated players into offensive roles. There is an urgency about the game, which considering the humid playing conditions, is impressive. The more experienced players attempt to set-up their nominated players with goal-scoring opportunities and use the limited space on the flanks to cross the ball into the centre with greater frequency. The nominated players are reinvigorated and work conscientiously during the game. They attempt to 'crash' the respective goal areas. Several players have also discovered that by delaying a run towards the opponents' goal momentarily often means that defenders will be unable to react to a cross, played back to a trailing attacker, because they are preoccupied with the most advanced player closest to goal. The change, prompted by the coach, appears to have impacted play in an attempt to facilitate the game (Thorpe & Bunker, 2008). Both teams benefitted from the modified game as indicated in their debriefing session. In response to the question 'Why were you successful in your final game?' the players noted via group discussion how attacking down the flanks, even on a small field, opened up playing space in the centre for offensive movement creating higher quality goal scoring opportunities for more players.

Knowledge for game-based coaching

In order to facilitate the session, the coach utilised an array of pedagogical strategies that emerge from a foundation of varied types of content knowledge. The first element is common content knowledge (CCK) that includes knowledge of game etiquette, rules, tactics and skills, frequently obtained through playing participation in the sport activity (Ward, 2009). For example, the coach recognised the varied team formations used during the small-sided game. Second, specialised content knowledge (SCK) represents learning tasks and game progressions to teach tactics and skills (Ward, 2009). In this case, beginning with a 4 versus 4 soccer game provided an initial manifestation of the adult game that opened the possibility of players encountering any of eight tactical principles of invasion game play – four offensive (advancement, mobility, width and depth) and four defensive (engagement, contraction, expansion and depth) as a potential basis for session development (Turner, 2014). SCK also includes the coach's ability to diagnose critical factors and common errors in performance (Ward, Piltz & Lehwald, 2018); for example, game play was compressed due to an increase in numbers of players in the game activity, prompting the coach to suggest goalkeepers might remain close to their respective goals as shot stoppers in order to help the game function effectively in the space available (see Turner & Ward, 2018, for an overview of the coach's soccer CCK and SCK). The institution of a two-point goal awarded to specific players represented the coach's understanding of different children's capabilities in the collective game situation based on observation of play. The quality of player performance was potentially improved as the previously predominant goal-scorers opted to become creators of scoring opportunities for less experienced players and vice versa. The coach's SCK is paired with what is known about specific players and the context for learning. Amending the modified game scoring structure to cater for differing age and ability levels in an attempt to improve play under oppressive heat conditions, where younger players were tiring is an example of the coach's Pedagogical Content Knowledge (PCK; Ward & Lehwald, 2018).

Game focusing and shaping incorporating constraints

The use of a small-sided conditioned game was part of the coach's toolkit (Turner, 2014) based on PCK. It was used to 'shape play' (Launder & Piltz, 2013, p. 60) and impact the game objective via the manipulation of a specific task constraint (stratified scoring). In addition to varying the goal of the game, task constraints also include manipulation of rules and equipment used during the game learning experience (Renshaw, Chow, Davids & Hammond, 2010), and the size four soccer ball was used to accommodate the younger players in the game, without detracting from the success of the older players. Another task constraint impacting the soccer game was the increase in playing numbers from four to six per team over the duration of the session. The players were able to utilise short distance passing and moving combinations and dribbling skills to evade opponents in a restricted space. Their 'game sense' in small-sided soccer was challenged in a tactically more complex game in the same playing area (Pill, 2012; Pill, 2013). If deemed appropriate, the coach could have altered the field dimensions to provide more space; more likely if game performance had declined due to an increase in team numbers (Turner, 2005). The coach also could have created a second goal close to the touchline at each end of the field for teams to attack by varying another constraint – the equipment (i.e., additional goals were available). Such a change may potentially have caused players to contemplate the use of width in attack. Instead, the coach challenged the teams to solve a tactical problem (via his question) that prompted one team to utilise two wide players to receive short passes from their goalkeeper. Via the question the coach encouraged the teams to 'focus' (Launder & Piltz, 2013) on an issue that emerged in the game as a 'teaching moment' (Turner & Martinek, 1995, p. 59).

If two more players had arrived, and joined the game, the coach may have considered using two smaller games (4 versus 4 and 3 versus 3), as a principle of game based coaching is using the smallest number of players to participate in the game to permit maximal opportunities to interact with the ball while maintaining the tactical complexity of the adult game (Turner, 2005). As the coach contemplated a change in the game structure the players initiated a negotiation with the coach to remain in a larger-sided game (6 versus 6) – also a common student negotiation in physical education between teachers and students who aim to modify instruction (Wahl-Alexander, Curtner-Smith & Sinelnikov, 2018). While some negotiations may be negative, aimed at making the game experience less demanding, the players perceived the 6 versus 6 game as more challenging and appropriate to their skill level. Experienced activity facilitators are able to recognise a positive player-initiated negotiation designed to improve the quality of the learning experience (Tsangaridou & O'Sullivan, 2003) and provide subtle advice to facilitate players' performances, such as employing the goalkeepers as shot-stoppers rather than sweeper-keepers helped to create more space on the field in the 6 versus 6 game – the coach responding to the players with a subtle tactical re-negotiation. Within game-based learning, areas of focus are often unpredictable and emergent. In this case it provided the players with an opportunity for input into their game context. Both shaping and focusing play are powerful implements in a coach's toolbox for use in small-sided games to enhance player decision-making and impact game performance (Ward et al., 2018).

Facilitating thoughtful game performers

By restricting interference in a game that primarily belonged to the players (they created the boundaries, self-refereed and did not use substitutes throughout the session) the coach attempted to protect the integrity of their game. By providing the players ownership of the game and allowing them to make multiple decisions the coach attempted to foster empowerment and an appreciation of the soccer game in the players (Cooper, 2010); key tenets of an athlete-centred approach to coaching and learning games (Kidman & Lombardo, 2010). As part of game-based learning, under an athlete-centred approach, the use of questioning is integral to stimulating player thinking, enhancing decision-making and facilitating problem solving. In Game Sense coaching, for example, the coach either constructs a game requiring players to use a tactical principle to solve a specific problem (convergent thinking) or from out of the game context players attempt to find a solution requiring divergent thinking or tactical creativity (Pill, 2018). The use of a questioning protocol (*what? where? when? why? with whom? how?*) has been suggested as a viable pedagogical tool in game-based approaches (Turner, 2005). *What* or *where* questions tend to be (lower order) factual and convergent leading to an established answer. They represent a response that the coach wants to hear and present knowledge as fixed rather than an exploration of possibilities (Forrest, 2014). Higher order questions (*how or why*) are divergent and encourage players to apply, analyse, synthesise and evaluate during game-based learning (Kidman & Lombardo, 2010). Coach Jimmy asked, 'How will your team set up to incorporate additional team members?' and 'Why were you successful in your final game?' In response to open-ended questions there are no correct or incorrect answers. In answering the initial question, after discussion within their groups, each team arrived at a different formation solution. This process also aligns with recent work undertaken on metacognition (thinking about thinking) in tactical game situations in volleyball during physical education classes (Chatzipanteli, Digelidis, Karatzoglidis & Dean, 2016). In this soccer scenario, players were monitoring progress to a solution to a game problem, but were also considering alternative solutions and potential adjustments via their ensuing discussion. Players were able to learn through questioning and problem solving, then providing a movement response to test and evaluate their strategy during the game (Kidman & Lombardo, 2010). The second question posed at the conclusion of the session, provided an opportunity for the players to think and reflect on their understanding generated during the final game.

Conclusion

The structure of this game-based soccer coaching scenario may be approximated to a Game Sense Pedagogy (Light, 2013). The players understood the initial game and participated in it, the coach questioned the players to identify a potential game problem and through team discussion the children devised strategies to formulate a response; they employed potential solutions in their game and then were able to reflect on their successes/weaknesses, and before playing again consider revisions. Light (2013) suggested that 'this sequence is not at all prescriptive and should be open to change according to the learners and the situation at hand' (p. 54). Accordingly, in the soccer session there was an additional intervention (stratified scoring) initiated by the coach in the final 10 mins based on observations of the players' performances and the context of the game (Turner, 2018). The coach viewed it as an opportunity to improve the quality of play further for all participants in the final game and attempted to facilitate player involvement. If a coach knows the game and content pedagogy, how to solicit participant input and can assist players via focusing and shaping play (including potential game constraints), then game-based coaching represents an invaluable approach in helping players to learn to play games.

References

Chatzipanteli, A., Digelidis, N., Karatzoglidis, C. & Dean, R. (2016). A tactical-game approach and enhancement of metacognitive behaviour in elementary school students. *Physical Education and Sport Pedagogy*, 21(2), 169–184.

Cooper, P. (2010). Play and children. In L. Kidman & B. J. Lombardo (eds), *Athlete-centred coaching: Developing decision makers* (2nd ed., pp. 137–150). Worcester: IPC Print Resources.

Forrest, G. (2014). Questions and answers: Understanding the connection between questioning and knowledge in game-centred approaches. In R. L. Light, J. Quay, S. Harvey & A. Mooney (eds), *Contemporary developments in games teaching* (pp. 167–177). New York: Routledge.

Kidman, L. & Lombardo, B. J. (2010). *Athlete-centred coaching: Developing decision makers* (2nd ed.). Worcester: IPC Print Resources.

Launder, A. & Piltz, W. (2013). *Play practice: Engaging and developing skilled players from beginner to elite*. Champaign, IL: Human Kinetics.

Light, R. (2013). *Game sense: Pedagogy for performance, participation and enjoyment*. New York: Routledge.

Pill, S. (2012). Teaching game sense in soccer. *Journal of Physical Education, Recreation and Dance*, 83(3), 42–46.

Pill, S. (2013). *Play with purpose: Game sense to sport literacy*. Hindmarsh, SA: ACHPER Publications.

Pill, S. (2018). Developing thinking players: A coach's experience with Game Sense coaching. In S. Pill (ed.), *Perspectives on Athlete-Centred Coaching* (pp. 93–103). New York: Routledge.

Renshaw, I., Chow, J., Davids, K. & Hammond, J. (2010). A constraints-led perspective to understanding skill acquisition and game play: A basis for integration of motor learning theory and physical education praxis? *Physical Education and Sport Pedagogy*, 15(2), 117–137.

Thorpe, R. D. & Bunker, D. (2008, May). *Teaching Games for Understanding: Do current developments reflect original intentions?* Paper presented at the

Fourth International Conference Teaching Games for Understanding, Vancouver, British Columbia, Canada.

Tsangaridou, N. & O'Sullivan, M. (2003). Physical education teachers' theories of action and theories in use. *Journal of Teaching in Physical Education*, 22, 132–152.

Turner, A. P. (2005). Teaching and learning games at the secondary level. In J. Butler & L. Griffin (eds), *Teaching Games for Understanding: Theory, research, and practice* (pp. 71–89). Champaign, IL: Human Kinetics.

Turner, A. P. (2014). Learning games concepts by design. In R. L. Light, J. Quay, S. Harvey & A. Mooney (eds), *Contemporary developments in games teaching* (pp. 193–196). New York: Routledge.

Turner, A. P. (2018). Athlete-centred coaching and Teaching Games for Understanding – Not quite the perfect match. In S. Pill (ed.), *Perspectives on athlete-centred coaching* (pp. 127–136). New York: Routledge.

Turner, A. P. & Martinek, T. J. (1995). Teaching for understanding: A model for improving decision-making during game play. *Quest*, 47, 44–63.

Turner, A. P. & Ward, P. (2018). Teaching sport skills – Soccer. In P. Ward & H. Lehwald (eds), *Effective physical education content and instruction: An evidence based and teacher-tested approach* (pp. 109–166). Champaign, IL: Human Kinetics.

Wahl-Alexander, Z., Curtner-Smith, M. & Sinelnikov, O. (2018). Influence of a training program on preservice teachers' ability to negotiate with students. *Journal of Teaching in Physical Education*, 37(2), 144–153.

Ward, P. (2009). Content matters: Knowledge that alters teaching. In L. Housner, M. Metzler, P. Schempp & T. Templin (eds), *Historic traditions and future directions of research on teaching and teacher education in physical education* (pp. 345–356). Morgantown, WV: Fitness Information Technology.

Ward, P. & Lehwald, H. (2018). *Effective physical education content and instruction: An evidence based and teacher-tested approach*. Champaign, IL: Human Kinetics.

Ward, P., Piltz, W. & Lehwald, H. (2018). Unpacking games teaching: What do teachers need to know? *Journal of Physical Education, Recreation and Dance*, 89(4), 39–44.

9 Teaching players to think the game
Beyond decision-making

Carlos Eduardo Gonçalves, Serge Éloi and Humberto M. Carvalho

Games are instrumental in sport training. We use them either for tactical purposes, for physical conditioning, or just for fun. This combination and interaction of effects is transversal to almost all games and represents an important part of the training sessions. However, and paradoxically, the motor, mental and affective richness of the game can induce a lack of conceptual clarity and an absence of purpose in the choice, design and implementation of the game: all games are good, and games are good to everything. From an epistemological and practical point of view this is particularly misleading because if a coach wants to teach how to play a game, it is not enough just to play it.

Our first argument is that coaches matter and that the good use of games as a teaching tool depends of good ideas, proper planning and careful instructions and corrections. In a study with basketball under-16 male teams, Gonçalves, Martins and Carvalho (2017) found that all the coaches, independently from experience or competitive level, considered that in every game players practice their decision-making skills. And in a recent unpublished academic study with basketball under-16 female teams, Maia and Gonçalves (2019) found that players from different teams have different opinions about what is needed to make good decisions in games, reflecting the priorities of their respective coaches.

Here we focus on the use of games in practice to foster the ability to understand the tactics of a specific sport that in many cases differ, in number of players, rules, size of the pitch, from that game. The concept of tactical learning refers to the players' capacity to build a coherent mental representation of the time and space of the game. However, the real content of teaching the 'tactics' is an intangibility that escapes to a clear definition suitable for all contexts. Furthermore, actual elite players are expected to be problem solvers in dynamical situations and in interaction with teammates and opponents. According to this premise, coaches should provide opportunities for their players to analyse, interpret and decide about the content of their training process (Butler, 2016).

Our second argument is that games do not teach how to make decisions, they just provide the context for the players to see what is happening and learn how to deal appropriately with fast-pace-everchanging situations. To this end, as Mulhern (2018) puts it, all seeing is ordinary and none is natural. In fact, 'ordinary' seeing must be educated to see the game through communication and consistent learning - and to 'see' is the first step to think the game.

One additional problem is the contemporary quest for creativity, which is pervasive of all human agency. Hence, athletes must be creative, and the best are the most creative ones, meaning that youth coaches must work to develop creativity among the talented players (Memmert, 2015). However, the work of Gopnik (2016) demonstrated that human development seems to be a trade-off between plasticity and efficiency. As we become more efficient at making decisions, we gradually lose our capacity to be creative and absorb the things that don't fit with what we know. As players improve their skills and accumulate hours of training, they 'see' the game better and are more able to make the right decision.

Our third and final argument is that it is time to stop mixing beginners, advanced and elite players. Every developmental stage presents different challenges and the games must be designed, taught and assessed accordingly. The tactical meaning of a small-sided game is best perceived by expert players, who can figure out the activity's ultimate purpose (Hodge, Henry & Smith, 2014). Recent interventions with beginners highlight the players' technical fragilities as a limit to the full exploitation of the pedagogical value of games (Santos & Morgan, 2019). Coaches know that what is tactically desirable must be physically and technically possible.

From theory to practice

One of the limitations of existent empirical studies about tactical thought and decision making in practice and competition is the almost exclusive focus on elite teams or athletes enrolled in a specialisation path to elite level. Some coaches continue to think that younger players do not possess enough knowledge to think about the game or express their opinions (Partington, Cushion & Harvey, 2014). However, if we accept that tactical skills are decisive for success in games, then it cannot exist in a specific age to begin with their teaching and learning. We believe that to coach the game is more than teaching decision-making and a plurality of resources can be used during all the stages of participation in games. We also believe that the role of the coach as a planner, mentor and provider of contents and keys for their interpretation is fundamental. We will provide practical examples of team sports to create, implement and develop pragmatic tools to help the players to love and think the game later in the chapter.

Games as pedagogical technology

This approach is based on four points: a goal, a method, knowledge built using devices and proposals for dissemination in the professional community. It is also important to note that when we mention techniques or technicality, we mean the competencies and skills, technical or tactical, which are necessary to play the games with a sufficient level of proficiency.

When we try to define goals, by recovering data from the field in the real world situations of sports action, the prerequisite is always to create the conditions for a useful proposal for practitioners or significant others. So, we must not stick to the scientific premises, but also consider mechanisms and alternatives of action whose technological validity has showed to be relevant.

The technological method consists of feeding the records of technicalities through the use of artefacts. The technological approach aims to confirm results by proposing a qualitative assessment. To categorise the expectations of technological research on physical and sport practices (PSP), we use the discriminating filter of the registers of technicality (register of mastery, reading, transformation and participation) in the observed interactions.

Motor and sports practices are imbued with techniques. Thus, the athlete integrates techniques that facilitate, through sensitive experience, the attainment of a certain degree of technicality. We propose a pedagogical approach to the appropriation of sports techniques that articulates the consideration of the individual in the specificity of his motor skills, on the one hand, and the educational intervention of the teacher or coach on the other hand (Clot, 1997; Durey 1997; Bouthier, 1997; Bouthier & Durey, 1994).

In the field of PSP, technical records can be classified by their different characteristics (Uhlrich, Éloi & Bouthier, 2011):

- the master's level that takes into account the state of mastery of sports skills;
- the reading level which covers the way in which the subjects involved in the practice are collecting information;

- the transformation level which refers to the conditions and procedures for the evolution of technical knowledge, the way how athletes take ownership of their decisions, as well as their development trajectory; and
- the level of participation, which is part of the activity deployed outside the main practice of the specific sport (e.g. when the athlete assumes the roles of referee, manager or observer).

Thus, the coach or researcher who is interested in the mobilisation of the techniques of the volleyball player goes into the device set up, investigating the level of the players' mastery (Éloi & Uhlrich, 2013). Thinking about technicality also means taking into account the reading of ball trajectories. The technological perspective envisages the functioning of the subject (athletes, stakeholders, coach, and researcher) in its relationship to the technical tools that surround him/her. Following the proposals of various authors (Cole, 1990, Norman, 1993; Rabardel, 1995; Vérillon, 2005) we now turn to the concept of artefacts.

'The anthropological notion of artefact refers to everything that has undergone a transformation, however minimal, of human origin' (Rabardel 1995, p. 59). It appears that the categories of artefacts that are most often used in the field of PSP can be defined as follows (Éloi & Uhlrich, 2013):

- Cognitive artefacts that are artificial and conceptual elements designed to
- process information in order to satisfy a representational function (Cole, 1990; Norman, 1993).
- Corporeal artefacts that occur when subjects mobilise elements of tactico-technical actions in line with their perception of the situation.
- Material artefacts that give new powers to practitioners, allowing them to possess the means to reorient their action.
- Regulatory artefacts that consist of a temporary amendment to the rules, as the coach causes incidents in body productions by disturbing for example the balance between the power of attack and defence; these transient transformations then offer new perspectives to the players of the game.

Traditionally in PSP, we only considered tools for changing the existing landscape or to help or to hamper the realisation of the motor task. There are also the established observational tools. We must definitely go beyond this fixed representation of what are the techniques or tools, in order to include them in the category of artefacts (Éloi & Uhlrich, 2011; Uhlrich, Éloi & Bouthier 2011). In this dynamic approach, we characterise the artefact as a voluntary incident in the activity of the subject in order to provoke a change in his/her motion patterns and to develop his/her skills. We then question the influence of the artefact on the activity of the subject, but in turn we take into account that the subjects' agency has the potential to transform the artefact. This interaction with the artefact applies to both the athletes as well as to the coaches.

This dynamic process suggests that the training to read the game (the observer's point of view) can be reinvested in the game (the player's point of view).

The game-based approach and the instrumental genesis

The technological approach only makes sense if disseminated among the coaches' and researchers' community by sharing experiences, results and reflexions. The use of games as technology needs to be tested in different contexts as part of an instrumental genesis (Rabardel, 1995; Éloi & Uhlrich, 2011). This pedagogical process requires a double movement. First, the instrumentation phase, or the period during which the athlete confronts the instrument/game proposed by the coach, tests its properties and experiences what the tool allows him/her to achieve. Instrumentation refers to a process oriented towards the athlete him/herself. This period involves various grouping and experiments, which is most often carried out through trial and error.

The next phase that overlaps with parts of the previous one, encompasses the period during which the athlete contributes to the evolution of the artefact. This is the period of instrumentalisation that contemplates the shift to the stage when the athlete constructs a repository of the appropriate or ineffective responses. This phase requires more technical proficiency and tactical instructions. Instrumentalisation is a process directed towards the artefact, concerning its utility, contradictions and evolution. Here, the athlete's power for innovation is expressed through a process of personalising the artefact in order to adapt it to his/her own use. This distinction of two complementary periods allows the coach to have a glimpse on the process of instrumental genesis as a plurality of transformations whose purposes are distinct or even antagonistic, albeit complementary. Vygotski's instrumental theory can be a useful intellectual guide through the concepts of sign, consciousness or experience (Vygotski, 2014).

The practice: Two examples

In volleyball, a game is 2 against 2 (1 + 1). Each duo can touch the ball a maximum of three times to put the ball into the opponents' court: the ball can, however, be returned directly or after two touches. In our situation, the game's governing laws are those of volleyball, but a new rule is introduced. The player who returns the ball into the opponents' court will be momentarily considered 'dead'. To get a new 'life' and continue to participate in the game, the player concerned must touch one of the two marker cones, which are located in the two angles at the back of the court. During the time when the 'dead' player is attempting to touch a marker cone, the other player in the team is alone to defend their full court.

What the coach is looking for is a succession of predictable situations where one side outnumbers the other (2 against 1), without influencing the unpredictable positioning of the opposing player left alone. The predictability of the situation when one side outnumbers the other is caused because all the actors know that the player returning the ball into the opponents' court is temporarily out of the game. The unpredictability is relative to the freedom of movement and position of the defender who remains alone during the short period of time. Assimilating information is encouraged by the certitude that there are determining factors of space and positioning to be recognised. However, everything happens within a short period of time, as the team in offense takes advantage of the temporary superiority and play the ball accordingly. Besides the physical and technical constraints, the coach is interested in the decisional constraint, which involves translating the assimilated information concerning the opponent into a tactical choice regarding the alternatives of attacking the opponents' court or making a pass to the partner. The role of the coach is to understand when to intervene to help the athletes to see and interpret what is happening in front of them. Depending of the context, the education of seeing and consequently, of the ability to make a good decision, takes time and the deliberate action of the coach.

In basketball, a fast-break situation of 4 against 3 (+ 1) or 3 against 2 (+ 1) is a common game situation. Like in the volleyball example, when a team recovers the ball possession, one of the defence players is 'dead' and must touch a pre-determined mark to be able to continue to play. The temporary advantage of the offense is predictable but not the defensive reaction. Because of the high speed of the game, it is hard to collect information and make the right choice. Once again, the coach must find a balance between the need to guide the players to see and make the good decision and when to let the athletes find and discover the possibilities of the game.

It is always about teaching and learning

The two simple examples presented above are artefacts, they are not the specific sport, and nothing guarantees that the abilities assimilated in practice are transferable to competitive settings. But, as we stressed above, sport is not always about high performance. Most of the participants in organised sport do not reach elite levels of competition. Nevertheless, it is the coaches' mission to teach their athletes to understand and play the game the best they can.

For Richards, Mascarenhas and Collins (2009, 2012) tactical apprenticeship would represent a kind of slow learning able to boost the development of good individual and team decisions in game situations through the elaboration of a shared mental model. Although we share a critical view of the concept of mental models, because of the diversity of people and contexts, we still think that it is a helpful theoretical position to understand the decision-making process. Some athletes will reach a very high level but only if they can 'see' the game and establish a competitive dialogue with their teammates and opponents. Other players do not have the physical and skill competencies to match their understanding of the game. This is a conclusion that comes only at the end of a long process of specialisation.

Game-based coaching: A challenge for research

Better understanding of game-based coaching approaches is key for developing practice. Diverse pedagogical approaches have been proposed, often sharing key similarities, including their holistic perspective. It is not our intention to enter the debate about the right theoretical framework to teach sport skills. Earlier we mentioned that we follow critically the concepts of Vygotski about human development and education. We consider that the coach is not a facilitator or an orchestrator but above all a teacher that cares about the nature of learning activities undertaken by each individual learner. However, we contend that game-based approaches have been under investigated. Most of the available information into the coaching process have elicited an incomplete understanding of the respective pedagogies due to deficiencies in the methodology, and likely more importantly, due to a narrow view of the process mostly focused on the coach. In games there are different levels of understanding of the relationship between technical proficiency and the ability to play the game efficiently. It is at this point that the question of technology, tools, and artefacts becomes crucial: How to teach? What kinds of resources are available or are suitable to facilitate the understanding of the game and help players to develop into ever-higher levels? How to transform a game into a coaching artefact? How can the coach foster the cognitive appropriation of coaching artefacts by the athletes?

The evolution of the impact of artefacts from a cognitive stage, when the athlete is only able to gather and interpret the available information, to an embodied stage, when the athlete engages in innovative technical and tactical actions resulting from his/her new perception of the game situation, can last for several years. The transition to an instrumental stage, when athletes are confident in their new competencies, allowing them to perform alternative actions, is possible only to the talented ones. By contrast, other players remain at the reading level and are not able to reach other performative stages (Richards, Collins & Mascarenhas, 2012).

Given the holistic perspective of game-based coaching, there is the need to explore the interactions between individual learners/athletes exposed and responding to the coaches' intervention, within the different learning environments. Games are a powerful tool to teach and learn sport, but only if they are more than just a 'funny' or athletic drill. Vygotski's instrumental theory, namely through the concepts of sign, conscience or experience, provides the intellectual ground for the use of coaching artefacts and for the evaluation of their utility. The development of the human capacity to imagine, create and innovate reaches its peak during adolescence. In our specific field of sport training, games can represent a good path to nurture and drive the athletes' imagination towards good decision-making in sport and in life

References

Bouthier, D. (1997). L'EPS et son rapport aux techniques. Spécial didactique; L'EPS dans l'école et la société d'aujourd'hui [The relationship between PE and technics]. *Spirales*, 8, 96–98.
Bouthier, D. & Durey, A. (1994). Technologie des activités physiques et sportives [Technology of physical activity and sport]. *Impulsions*, 1, 117–126.
Butler, J. (2016). *Playing fair: Using student-invented games to prevent bullying, teaching democracy, and promote social justice.* Champaign, IL: Human Kinetics.
Clot, Y. (1997). Technique et travail humain. Spécial didactique; L'EPS dans l'école et la société d'aujourd'hui [Technology and human labour]. *Spirales*, 8, 90–93.

Cole, A. (1990). Cultural psychology, a once and future discipline? In J. J. Berman (ed.), *Current theory and research in motivation, 37. Nebraska Symposium on Motivation, 1989: Cross-cultural perspectives* (pp. 279–335). Lincoln, NE: University of Nebraska Press.

Durey, A. (1997). L'EPS et son rapport à la technique [The relationship between PE and technics]. *Spirales*, 8, 93–95.

Éloi, S. & Uhlrich, G. (2011). La démarche technologique en STAPS: analyse conceptuelle et mise en perspective pour les sports collectifs [The technological process in team sports]. *eJRIEPS*, 23, 20–45.

Éloi, S., Uhlrich, G. (2013). La mobilisation d'un artefact réglementaire dans le cadre de la formation d'étudiants en STAPS. Une illustration en volleyball [A rule artefact in PETE: the case of Volleyball]. *Recherche et formation*, 73, 73–88.

Gonçalves, C. E., Martins, A. M. & Carvalho, H. M. (2017). Inovação pedagógica no Basquetebol jovem:missão difícil mas necessária [Pedagogical Innovation in youth Basketball: an urgent and hard mission]. *Revista Euroamericana de Ciencias del Deporte*, 6(supl.), 157–162.

Gopnik, A. (2016). *The gardener and the carpenter*. New York: Farrar, Straus and Giroux.

Hodge, K., Henry, G. & Smith, W. (2014). A case study of excellence in elite sport: Motivational climate in a world champion team. *The Sport Psychologist*, 28(1), 60–74.

Lebed, F. & Bar-Eli, M. (2014). *Complexity and control in team sports*. Abingdon: Routledge.

Maia, J. & Gonçalves, C. E. (2019). Efeitos da experiência de jogo sobre a tomada de decisão em Basquetebol: estudo com jogadoras sub16 [Effects of sport experience on decision making in Basketball: a study with female under-16 players]. Unpublished master's thesis, University of Coimbra, Portugal.

Memmert, D. (2015). *Teaching tactical creativity in sport*. London: Routledge.

Mulhern, F. (2018). Critical revolutions. *New Left Review*, 110, 39–56.

Norman, D. A. (1993). Les artefacts cognitifs. *Raisons Pratiques*, 4, 15–34.

Partington, M., Cushion, C. J. & Harvey, S. (2014). An investigation of the in-game behaviours of professional, top-level youth soccer coaches. *Journal of Sports Sciences*, 32(5), 403–414.

Rabardel, P. (1995). *Les hommes et les technologies: Approche cognitive des instruments contemporains*. Paris: Armand Colin.

Richards, P., Collins, D. & Mascarenhas, D. (2012) Developing rapid high-pressure team decision-making skills. The integration of slow deliberate reflective learning within the competitive performance environment: A case study of elite netball. *Reflective Practice*, 13(3), 407–424.

Richards, P., Mascarenhas, D. & Collins, D. (2009) Implementing reflective practice approaches with elite team athletes: parameters of success, *Reflective Practice*, 10(3), 353–363.

Santos, M. & Morgan, K. (2019). Developing creative team games players: from jazz to sport coaching. *International Journal of Sports Science & Coaching*, 14(2), 117–125.

Uhlrich, G., Éloi, S. & Bouthier, D. (2011). La technologie dans le contexte des STAPS: de la conception d'outils à la conceptualisation... et réciproquement. [Technology in the context of sport: from tool design to the concepts]. *eJRIEPS*, 23, 4–19.

Vérillon, P. (2005). Processus productifs et constructifs dans les activités physiques et sportives: la place de l'instrument [Productive and constructive processes in PA and sport]. *Impulsions*, 4, 305–325.

Vygotski, L. (1986). *Thought and language*. Cambridge, MA: MIT Press.

Vygotski, L. (2004). Imagination and creativity in childhood. *Journal of Russian and East European Psychology*, 42(1), 7–97.

Vygotski, L. (2014). *Histoire du développement des fonctions psychiques supérieures*. [History of the development of central psychic functions]. Paris: La Dispute.

10 Exploring pedagogical tensions
Providing practical examples for tennis coaches to navigate a shift to game-based coaching

Mitch Hewitt and Shane Pill

The evolution of contemporary instructional practices for sport coaching share common and complementary pedagogical features which include an intent to develop 'thinking players' through game-based practice. Research has demonstrated that despite a desire to align with a Game Sense approach (Australian Sports Commission, 1996), the instructional practices of Australian tennis coaches remain aligned to the more traditional pedagogical intent of developing and reproducing prescribed techniques associated and in conjunction with direct instruction (Hewitt, 2015). These practices have invariably positioned the coaches' focus on developing a player's technique largely in isolation and removed from the tactical aspects of the game. Under the conditions of direct instruction, the coach has been regarded as the 'sole source of knowledge and has been responsible for the unidirectional transmission of this information to athletes who have adopted a largely passive role in the teaching and learning process' (Jones, 2006, p. 43). However, in recognising that tennis players should be exposed to planned activities that foster development in four central domains, which include; the physical (technique), social (interaction), cognitive (decision-making) and affective (fun and enjoyment) domains, as opposed to primarily one central domain (i.e., the physical/technique), the Game Sense approach (den Duyn, 1997) for sport teaching acknowledges the benefits of incorporating a more game-based practice environment that promotes development in all domains.

Empirical insights into Australian tennis coaches' practice revealed that coaches expressed a desire to implement pedagogies that are more representative of a game-based approach. However, even when coaches believed they were acting as game-based coaches, the reality of their practice was still to command and direct player behaviour in a didactic and highly prescriptive way throughout coaching sessions (Hewitt, 2015). These findings strongly indicate incongruences and tensions between the current on-court practices of tennis coaches and their desire to employ game-based approaches. This chapter will outline these tensions, and then provide a series of practical examples that will guide coaches to adopt a 'toolkit' that emphasises representative activities relevant to the game; that is, the game modifications and designer games. These elements will serve to highlight learning through guided discovery and the encouragement of thinking, decision-making and problem solving to learn in and through play.

Tennis coaches and their instruction style

In the research conducted by Hewitt (2015) 208 tennis coaches were asked 'what' instructional practices, based on Mosston and Ashworth's (2008) Spectrum of Teaching Styles, they believed they were performing via a survey. Further, 12 coaches volunteered to participate in observation of their coaching sessions to determine 'what' instructional practices they were performing. In addition to these observations, an additional (thirteenth) coach participated in an extended observational period of 18 hours of coaching at their local tennis club. The third part of the study also explored the insights of the 13 coaches in connection to their coaching practices as well as the motivations that informed their decisions to employ particular 'ways' of coaching.

The findings from the survey questionnaire revealed that all coaches believed that they employed a range of coaching practices – including the predominant application of a game-based approach. The three commonly identified 'ways' of coaching consisted of a 'practice style', a 'command style' in addition to a 'guided-discovery style. A 'practice style' of coaching, is largely representative of developing, practicing and reproducing prescribed techniques under the direct instruction of the coach in addition to receiving private feedback about performance. A 'command style' form of coaching is commonly representative of a highly directive style focussed on the replication of coach instructions in a synchronised action (i.e., copying the actions of the coach). 'guided discovery', a teaching style often associated with game-based approaches to coaching, is associated with questioning and having players engage in problem solving under the guidance and facilitation of the coach. While the observational aspect of the research aligned with the coaches using a 'practice' and 'command' style of coaching, there was no evidence of the coaches implementing a 'guided discovery style' during their coaching sessions.

The third part of the study – interviews – identified and highlighted significant incongruences, a lack a clarity, awareness, understanding and application of implementing, during coaching sessions, the guiding features of a game-based approach. It was revealed that all the coaches believed that they coached in a 'way' consistent with the tenets of the Game Sense coaching approach. These included:

- Asking players to respond to questions about tactical and technical skills and challenges during practice;
- Allowing players to primarily engage in rallying and game play during practice;
- Not employing highly prescriptive practices (i.e., telling players what to do or how to do it); and
- Limiting ball feeding during practice.

During the interviews, coaches had trouble describing 'why' they coached in particular ways, and specifically 'why' the observed coaching was different to what they believed was their enacted coaching practice or approach (Pill, Hewitt & Edwards, 2016).

The study showed that Australian coaches use a limited range of coaching practices. Although tennis coaches articulated the distinctiveness of a game-based approach and believed their coaching to be congruent with this approach, congruence was not evident in their observed coaching. The interviews established that despite the coaches' limited awareness of the instructional practices they perform during coaching sessions, they voiced the type of environment that they primarily wished to produce, and the behaviours that they wanted to encourage, were those of a game-based coaching approach (Hewitt, 2015). The coaches identified that they did not alter their coaching practices based on the age or ability of the players they were coaching despite undertaking different activities. Catering to the developmental readiness of players via the concept of modification of activities is a central feature of a game-based approach (Australian Sports Commission, 1996).

Practical examples to guide coaches to adopt a game-based coaching 'instructional toolkit'

If tennis coaches wish to employ game-based practice, practical examples of game-based coaching together with an explanation of these practices are required. Rink (2001) explained, 'You don't want to know simply that something works – you want to know why it works' (p. 23). A key recommendation from the research conducted by Hewitt (2015) in addressing the incongruences between perceived and actual

Exploring pedagogical tensions 99

practices, was to provide a framework designed to assist coaches to navigate through the various elements of a game-based approach for greater understanding and application. The Game Sense model as play with purpose presented by Pill and SueSee in Chapter 1 assists this navigation. The key conceptual features of Pill and SueSee's model can be seen in Figure 10.1. A variety of tennis activities will now be presented designed to provide practical examples that represent each element of the Game Sense approach as play with purpose (Pill & SueSee, 2020).

Game 1: Groundstroke Scramble

The game 'Groundstroke Scramble' (Figure 10.1) provides an example of the initial 'Game 1' element illustrated in Pill and SueSee's play with

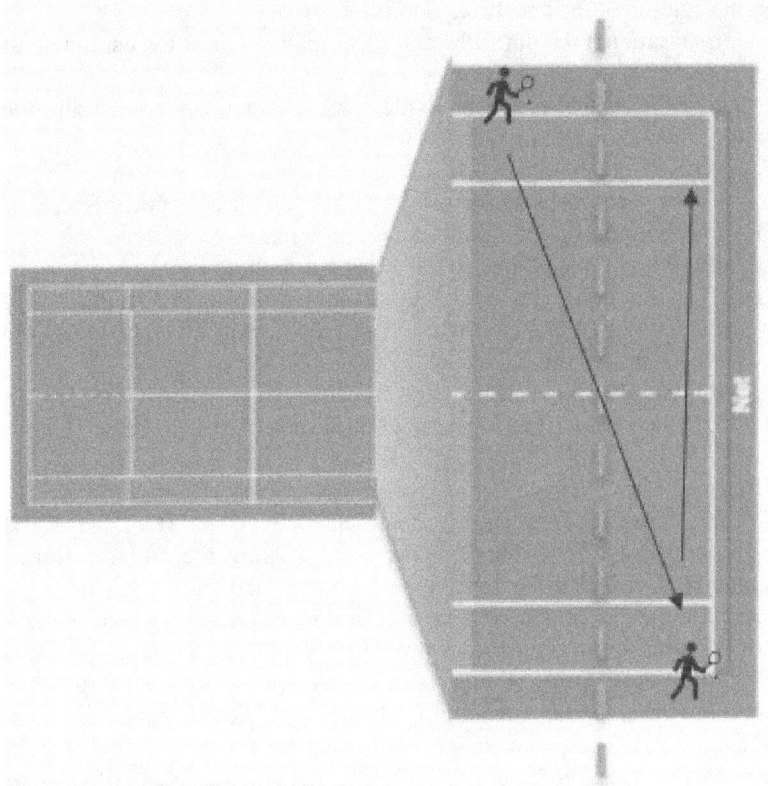

Figure 10.1 Groundstroke Scramble.

purpose explanation (Chapter 1). The central feature of the game of tennis – the rally (projection and reception of a ball), in combination with the technical skill of striking with a racquet and the relevant tactical elements associated with returning the ball and winning the point, are represented. The notion of representation – during the 'Game' element of a Game Sense Approach - is an important pedagogical aspect. The concept of representation suggests that each 'Game' played during a coaching session be representative of the key aspects or features of the game being practiced (Griffin, Butler & Sheppard, 2018). For instance, a fundamental principle of the game of tennis is the rally, which consists of the projection and reception of an object in a court area divided by two equal halves. As part of the game of 'Groundstroke Scramble' a combined tactical and technical problem is also posed for the players. Players are therefore challenged to consider the co-development of the technical and tactical aspects of the game. The game rules for 'Groundstroke Scramble' are:

Organisational layout: Players form pairs and are positioned at opposite ends of the court.

Tactical/technical problem: Explore ways to win the point using the width and length of the court.

a   Player 1 commences the rally with a drop hit or overarm serve
b   Players rally the ball until and error is made
c   Players are not permitted to volley the ball
d   The rally continues until the ball bounces twice before being hit, the ball lands outside the court space, the ball hits the net, or the player misses the ball
e   Players alternate commencing the point
f   Play first player to 10 points or until the coach calls 'time'

'Reflect'

When a 'teachable moment' is identified by the coach (Launder, 2001) or at the end of a defined period when playing the aforementioned game of 'Groundstroke Scramble', the coach has the option of engaging the players in the element referred to as 'Reflect' which is associated with questioning and problem-solving. Purposeful questions designed to promote problem solving and player engagement in the learning are a key tenet of the Game Sense approach (den Duyn, 1997). The pedagogical prominence on the coach's use of well-considered questions to create reflective moments, a debate of ideas or the guided discovery of tactical and technical concepts distinguishes the Game Sense approach from the more historically common directive 'sport as sport techniques' instruction (Kirk, 2010). An example of a series of questions related to the game of 'Groundstroke Scramble' during the 'Reflect' element of the Game Sense approach is listed below:

- Identify the type of shots and positions on the court you may hit the ball to attack?
- How might you position your opponent during the rally to win the point?
- What are the most desirable positions on the court to hit the ball in order to win the point?
- If your opponent is forced wide on the court, where might you hit the ball? What about if your opponent is close to the net?
- How do you position your body and racquet to control the direction of the ball?
- What are the implications of contacting the ball 'late' (level or behind your body) or early (in front of your body)?

Where to next? – A non-linear journey

At this point during a coaching session, the coach is presented with options in relation to which element of play with purpose (see Chapter 1, this volume) to engage players in. Considering that the model is 'non-linear' - in that a coach is not constrained by following a systematic or ordered step-by-step process in connection to the various elements representative of the Game Sense model - arguably, this decision aligns with Tomlinson's (1999) differentiated model. Tomlinson's model highlights the requirement for coaches to 'respond to the needs of all learners, with consideration being given to the student's readiness, interest, and capabilities' (Whipp, Taggart & Jackson, 2012, p. 12). For instance, some players may lack the required movement competence to continue to play 'Game 1' without a racquet modification, therefore, some type of equipment modification may be required to reduce the complexity of the technical skill challenge. Alternatively, a select number of players may require a focused and isolated practice episode on a particular technical or tactical aspect to further improve performance when playing 'Game 1'. Furthermore, some players may have achieved the requisite tactical and technical problems associated with 'Game 1' and are ready to be challenged by another technical and tactical concept – this would constitute moving to 'Game 2' in the Game Sense approach as play with purpose illustration shown in

Chapter 1. 'Game 2' would provide a different technical and tactical challenge, while still focussing on the target concept of the session.

'Modify'

Another element of the Game Sense approach is game modification (Australian Sports Commission, 1996). Modifying games permits sports coaches to highlight certain features of play, while retaining the essential elements of the game. The CHANGE IT formula (Figure 10.2; Schembri, 2005) serves to guide coaches in understanding how task, performer and environment constraints (Pill & Hewitt, 2017) structure the modification of games by 'eliminating, refining, or adding to game rules and playing conditions (such as field size) to focus attention on specific tactical or technical game understanding' (Pill, 2013, p. 9).

Game modification by exaggeration, elimination, or simplification (Australian Sports Commission, 1996) in tennis can be explained by a constraints-led perspective (Hewitt, Pill & McDonald, 2018). The deliberate design of games (Charlesworth, 1994) constrains the player to seek a movement option to achieve a movement strategy to resolve the constraint(s) that are applied (Davids, Button & Bennett, 2008). Regardless of 'lens' on the explanation, tennis coaches can modify and adapt the structure of games to foster, exaggerate or change player actions to develop responsive movements (Pill & Hewitt, 2017). Within a tennis context, for example, coaches may consider the following modifications:

C – coaching style

H – how to score

A – are or dimension of play space

N – number of players

G – game rules

E – equipment

I – inclusion by modification for learning needs

T – time (length) or the game/playing time or time permitted in possession

Figure 10.2 The CHANGE IT formula.
Source: Schembri (2005)

- the structure of games, including game rules, equipment and playing area in an attempt to exaggerate, eliminate, or enhance player movement during game play; and
- the application of modified activities that maintains the central tactical features of the game that appeals to the developmental readiness and individual needs of the player (Hewitt et al., 2018).

The element of 'Modify' in the Game Sense approach as play with purpose illustrated in Chapter 1 by Pill and SueSee can also be incorporated in 'Game 1' – 'Groundstroke Scramble' (Figure 10.1). For instance, whereas in the common form of tennis the ball is only permitted to bounce once in the court, players may be offered the choice of one or two bounces to play the ball based on where they determine their entry point lies during the game. Alternatively, players may have the option of first tapping the ball with the racquet to first control the ball, with or without letting the tapped ball bounce after being hit to gain control, before returning the ball to their opponent. Similarly, players may choose a lower compression ball – which travels through the air slower – in order to increase time to obtain a balanced body position prior to returning the ball over the net. Eliminating the use of racquets in favour of throwing and catching the ball during the game presents another entry level choice for players who may not have the physical or technical abilities to fulfil the tactical objectives of the game.

'Practice'

As outlined previously, tennis involves application of specific instructional practices to comprehensively develop the player across multiple learning domains. Consistent with athlete-centred tennis coaching (Hewitt, Edwards, Reid & Pill, 2018), coaches are encouraged to select practices that harmonise with several considerations and the intent of their instruction. For instance, there may be occasions when coaches want players to achieve consistency with regard to the execution of motor responses. In these instances, the coach might be more concerned with repetition of practice activities, developing the capacity to produce a motor response and individual learning than they are with more complex cognitive constructed learning or socialisation outcomes. In this case, implementing the element of 'Practice' from the Game Sense approach as play with purpose illustrated in Chapter 1 might be considered appropriate. Goldberger, Ashworth and Byra (2012) have suggested that this type of coaching presents as highly effective in

104 Hewitt and Pill

achieving 'basic' motor acquisition (Goldberger et al., 2012). The guiding features of a 'Practice' episode can be seen below in the activity called 'Jackpot' (Figure 10.3). In this activity, players are focused on cooperatively practicing a forehand groundstroke in a crosscourt direction with an emphasis on repetition of practice while receiving feedback from the coach. In this example, the purpose of the 'Practice' episode is to refine a specific technical and tactical skill – in this case - the forehand groundstroke in a crosscourt direction with control, accuracy and consistency. The game rules for 'Jackpot' are outlined below:

- **Organisational layout:** Players form pairs and are positioned at opposite ends of the court in a crosscourt (diagonal) position.

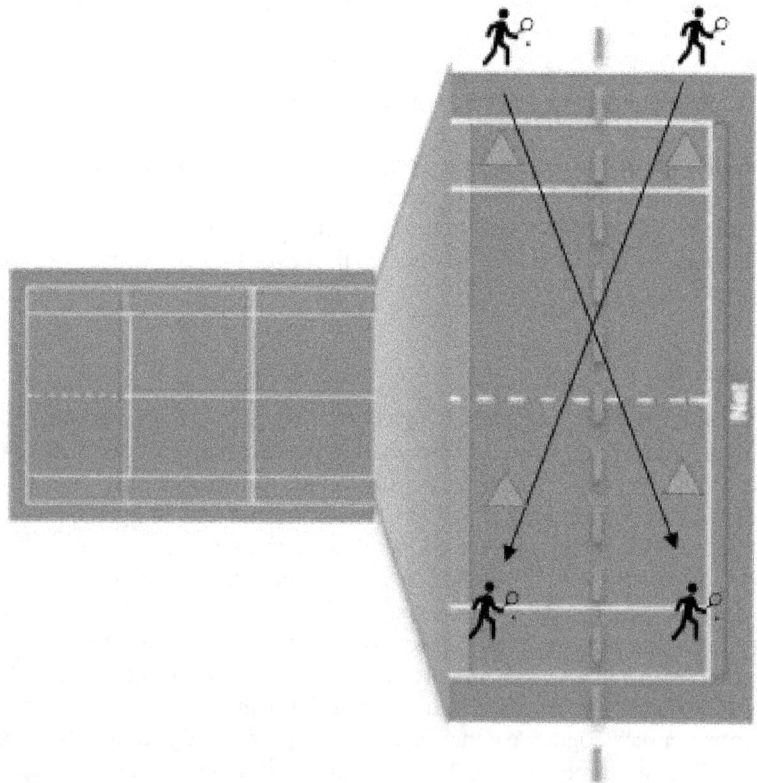

Figure 10.3 Jackpot – an activity for the 'Practice' element of the Game Sense approach as play with purpose.

- **Practice task:** Players are cooperatively practicing a forehand groundstroke in a crosscourt direction. Cones are positioned on the court for players to aim at.
  - a Students place cones to assist in control, direction and accuracy.
  - b Player 1 commences the rally by projecting the ball with a forehand drop hit in a crosscourt direction, aiming to land the ball as close to cones positioned at Player 2's end.
  - c Player 2 tracks the movement of the ball, allowing it to bounce once before returning the ball with a forehand in a crosscourt direction, aiming to land the return as close to the cones positioned at Player 1's end.
  - d Players continue to cooperatively practice hitting and rallying a forehand groundstroke in a crosscourt direction.

The duration of the 'Practice' episode is determined by the coach in relation to the player's performance and engagement. Within the pedagogical tenets of the Game Sense approach, the player would then return to playing 'Game 1' – 'Groundstroke Scramble' (Figure 10.1) to validate and 'test' the practiced skill in a competitive game scenario.

Conclusion

Despite tennis coaches in Australia predominantly implementing a 'practice style' of coaching during sessions, it is clear from research findings (Hewitt, 2015) that coaches are confronted with a level of uncertainty and understanding in connection as to 'how' to practically incorporate game-based coaching into their daily coaching endeavours in a manner that incorporates 'practice' episodes within coaching sessions when appropriate. It is important to acknowledge that the element of 'practice' within the Game Sense approach as play with purpose illustrated in Chapter 1 is a highly relevant option for coaches during practice (Farrow, 2010). Anecdotal reflections based on the authors' experience of tennis coaching over 30 years identifies the inclination of tennis coaches in Australia to elevate the priority toward the technical development of players, while philosophically coveting the guiding principles of a game-based approach – despite these principles often not being obvious or evident in their coaching.

References

Australian Sports Commission. (1996). *Game sense: perceptions and actions.* Research report. Belconnen, ACT: Australian Sports Commission.

Charlesworth, R. (1994). Designer games. *Sports Coach*, 17(4), 30–33.
Davids, K., Button, C. & Bennett, S. (2008). *Dynamics of skill acquisition: A constraints-led approach*. Champaign, IL: Human Kinetics.
Den Duyn, N. (1997). *Game sense: Developing thinking players: A presenter's guide and workbook*. Canberra, ACT: Australian Sports Commission.
Farrow, D. (2010). *Holistic skill development: Balancing technical and tactical needs*. Paper presented at the Conference of Science, Medicine & Coaching in Cricket, Melbourne, Australia, 12 July.
Goldberger, M., Ashworth, S & Byra, M. (2012). Spectrum of teaching styles retrospective 2012. *Quest*, 64, 268–282.
Griffin, L., Butler, J. & Sheppard, (2018). Extending the possibilities of a holistic and process oriented model to athlete development. In S. Pill (ed.), *Perspectives on athlete-centred coaching* (pp. 9–23). New York: Routledge.
Hewitt, M. (2015). *Teaching styles of Australian tennis coaches: An exploration of practices and insights using Mosston and Ashworth's Spectrum of Teaching Styles*. Unpublished Doctor of Philosophy thesis, School of Linguistics, Adult and Specialist Education, The University of Southern Queensland.
Hewitt, M., Edwards, K., Ashworth, S. & Pill, S. (2016). Investigating the teaching styles of tennis coaches using the Spectrum. *Sport Science Review*, 25(5/6), 321–344.
Hewitt, M., Edwards, K. & Pill, S (2016). Teaching styles of Australian junior tennis coaches. In J.Bruce & C. North (eds), *2015 Game Sense for Teachers and Coaches Conference proceedings* (pp. 40–52). Christchurch, 19–20 November.
Hewitt, M., Edwards, K., Reid, M. & Pill, S. (2018). Applying the game sense approach and Mosston and Ashworth's Inclusion Style E to promote athlete-centred tennis coaching with junior novice players. In S. Pill (ed.), *Perspectives on athlete-centred coaching* (pp. 93–103). New York: Routledge.
Hewitt, M., Pill, S. & McDonald, R. (2018). Informing game sense pedagogy with a constraints-led perspective for teaching tennis in schools. *Ágora para la Educación Física y el Deporte*, 20(1), 46–67.
Jones, R. (2006). *The sports coach as educator*. New York: Routledge.
Kirk, D. (2010). *Physical education futures*. Abingdon: Routledge.
Launder, A. G. (2001). *Play practice: The games approach to teaching and coachingsports*. Champaign, IL: Human Kinetics.
Mosston, M. & Ashworth, S. (2008). *Teaching physical education (1st online ed)*. Spectrum Institute for Teaching and Learning.
Pill, S. (2013). *Play with purpose: Game sense to sport literacy*. Hindmarsh, SA: ACHPER Publications.
Pill, S. & Hewitt, M. (2017). Tennis coaching: Applying the game sense approach. *Strategies: A Journal for Physical and Sport Educators*, 30(2), 10–16.
Pill, S., Hewitt, M. & Edwards, K. (2016). Exploring tennis coaches' insights in relation to their teaching styles. *Baltic Journal of Sport and Health Science*, 102(3), 30–43.

Pill, S. & SueSee. (2020). The Game Sense approach as play with purpose. In S. Pill (eds), *Perspectives on game-based coaching*. New York: Routledge.
Rink, J. E. (2001). Investigating the assumptions of pedagogy. *Journal of Teaching in Physical Education*, 20, 112–128.
Schembri, G. (2005). *Playing for life: Coach's guide*. Canberra, ACT: Australian Sports Commission.
Tomlinson, C. A. (1999). *The differentiated classroom: Responding to the needs of all learners*. Alexandria, VA: Association for Supervision and Curriculum Development.
Whipp, P., Taggart, A. & Jackson, B. (2012). Differentiation in outcome-focused physical education: pedagogical rhetoric and reality. *Physical Education and Sport Pedagogy*, 7(12), 1–11.

11 Exploring coach educators' experiences with developing game-based coaching

Shane Pill and Dave Reynolds

In this chapter we explore the idea that game-based coaching is accepted in coach education, policy and academic settings more than it is in the 'natural' setting of coaching. We draw on the concept of the sport coach as educator (Jones, 2006) and the idea of an 'everyday' philosophy of teaching developed by Green (1998, 2000a, 2002). Using a dialogue between two coach educators, who are also practicing coaches, we intentionally provoke an assumed acceptance of game-based coaching, and suggest that it is a conceptualised instructional approach, while coaches operate from an 'everyday' philosophy and pragmatic interpretation of a combination of instructional styles and 'what works' for them. This is because coaches do not need to see the boundaries between coaching approaches that coach educators and academics do as theory generators and explainers of theory (Green, 2000a; Stolz & Pill, 2016). To the coach educator and academic, the act of coaching can be viewed with an interpretation of the dynamics of the coaching setting, while for the coach, the practice of coaching is theoretically informed but made 'real' through the experience of coaching.

In order to position the coaches in the narrative, Coach Educator 1 (Duncan) believes that coaching is the 'art' of managing what is a frequently unpredictable pedagogical relationship between players and the coach working to achieve the outcomes of the game plan. This is a relationship that is more dynamic than adherence to pedagogical or instructional models (Metzler, 2011) that provide conceptualised 'blueprints' to follow allow. Coach Educator 2 (Cherie) has done postgraduate study in sport coaching and developed a conviction towards 'tactical' models of sport coaching (cf: Game Sense approach – Australian Sports Commission, 1996; Gréhaigne, Wallian & Godbout, 2005 – Tactical Decision Learning Model; Wein, 2004 – Game Intelligence).

It is a premise of this narrative that sport coaching is not a reductive process that can result in a 'blue-print' to follow. Coaching is instead multifaceted with the pedagogical acts of coaching and player learning forming an interactive complementarity with situational constraints (Jones, 2006, 2007). It is also a premise of this narrative that the essential characteristics of a tactical or game-based coaching style are different to that of mostly directive and reproductive style of coaching. Game-based coaching centrally organises training sessions by forms of game play and emphasise player development by guiding inquiry and discovery, whereas a directive and reproductive style of coaching centrally organises around content demonstration and prescription, and coach instruction that is highly controlling. The purpose is movement reproduction that is often decontextualised from game play at practice (Pill, 2012, 2015; Viciana & Mayorga-Vega, 2014).

The origin of this chapter is the various discussions over many years with coaches, coach educators, and academics that we have experienced and that often turn to discussion about the nature of various coaching approaches. Therefore, the intent of the narrative approach is to recapture many of the central themes discussed over the years in a format recognised as suitable for investigating conceptual debates (Jones, 2007; Stolz & Pill, 2014). The narrative approach adopted takes the form of a fictional dialogue similar to that used by Jones (2007), and Stolz and Pill (2014). The narrative not only attempts to reflect certain ideas prevalent in the extant literature, it is constructed to reach practitioners, to help them reflect and possibly change their practice by providing a way through which ideas can be accessed, shared and critically evaluated against the context of their own coaching experience (Armour, 2006; Stolz & Pill, 2014).

Contextualising the everyday reality of the sport coach

Whilst sitting in a café, meeting to discuss a coach education course the coming weekend.

DUNCAN: I am not sure we should be running with game sense and decision-making training as the main idea in the skill acquisition section of the course this weekend. We have been doing these courses for over ten years. The reality is these coaches still do a lot of reproduction drill-based work. They must value it and see it as useful otherwise I would have thought that we would have seen a shift in coaching practice to playing more games with purpose at training by now.

CHERIE: I understand what you are saying, and game-based approaches penetration into physical education teaching has attracted the same observation of acceptance in theory more than in practice (Stolz & Pill, 2014). I think many coaches see game-based coaching as game only training and that is why the approach faces resistance a lot of the time. I see it as our role to dispel the idea that game-based coaching is game only, or simply throw out the ball and let them play. A game form may be the focus of training (Australian Sports Commission, 1996). That is not the same as games are the only thing a coach implements at training.

DUNCAN: My problem with the idea of game-based coaching being the use of small sided or modified games is that this is not particularly new or innovative. I am old enough to remember attending workshops run by Eric Worthington in the 1970s. He used games to teach principles of play (Worthington, 1974). Coaches have been using these activities for a long time as part of their 'toolkit' of coaching styles.

CHERIE: I think yes, some have been using them for years, but I will challenge if the majority understand when and how to use games. In my observation as I get around the suburbs and watch community club coaching, many games are still only used by coaches after a series of 'skill drills' towards the back of training, or with junior teams they might play a game, not a version of the actual game itself, but something playful as just a warm-up activity. Mostly I see coaches not meeting a purpose other than 'it's a good warm-up activity', or with the use of game form training activities that they believe is a good way to finish training.

DUNCAN: I often see games used with no identified learning intention, coaches and players not understanding why they are doing it and understanding whether the game meets an objective the coach wants to focus on. Purposefully conditioning games, or changing constraints to align with a learning intention, is something that I think is still raw with coaches having limited understanding (Renshaw, Davids, Newcombe & Roberts, 2019).

CHERIE: That is surprising, as conditioning a game purposefully to focus on a strategy and tactical options has been emphasised as good coaching practice since Allen Wade's work in the 1960s (Wade, 1967). My own work is influenced by Rick Charlesworth's concept of designer games (Charlesworth, 1994). He emphasised designer games to teach tactical and technical components together. He was world coach of the year eight times (Charlesworth, 2016), so he must know a thing or two about good coaching.

DUNCAN: But techniques are important. Look at that goal by Eddie Betts the other night. Some coach scientists will come out and say, look at that adaptive flexibility to the need of the moment. The article in the paper quotes his teammates as saying he practices those sort of kicks at training (Greenwood, 2019). The techniques are in his 'movement toolkit'. We see 'time and time again' that these techniques do not simply emerge in the moment, and that they are a practiced skill.

CHERIE: But game-based coaching is not game-only coaching. There is still the warm-up where technical actions have the opportunity to be practiced and refined in closed and open drills. Additionally, there is the opportunity for small group and individualised practice in place of the warm-down laps at the end of the team practice component, which some coaches call 'craft work' (Pill, 2019). If a coach is using a Game Sense coaching approach, for example, players may be removed from the game form practice to work on a technique, before returning to the game to see if the practice has made a difference to their play. This was demonstrated in the Game Sense coaching videos (Coffee & den Duyn, 1997).

DUNCAN: Look, I have been coaching for 30 years, and in my experience, there is no 'holy grail' of pedagogies (Tinning, 2010). This inference that Game Sense coaching, or Tactical Games, or constraints-led coaching is superior, does not resonate with my experience of coaching. I am happy to go with game-based coaching as it is in the national delivery program we have to teach, but how is it better than going with a flexible approach where I plan my coaching session based on what I think the players need that week?

CHERIE: The problem with that smorgasbord approach (Stolz & Pill, 2016) is that the coaching will most likely lack learning coherence and connectedness, effecting players skill acquisition progression. I am not suggesting that all that be done is play purposeful games at training. Adopting the idea of the sport coach as educator (Jones, 2006), I agree with Mosston that both production and reproduction styles of teaching have a place (Mosston & Ashworth, 2002), as I explained earlier. What a game-based coaching approach does is give a framework for when those styles of teaching are used (Pill & SueSee, 2020).

DUNCAN: While I am at it, what is the difference between Game Sense coaching and constraints-led coaching? I was talking to a coach from the UK over here looking at some of the work we are doing, and she started to talk about a tactical approach. I have seen demonstrations of TGfU, a Tactical Games model, a Game Sense approach and a Game Intelligence approach at coaching conferences, and frankly, they all look the same when demonstrated at these coaching events.

CHERIE: The idea of deliberately conditioning the play to provide a game form that specifies a principle of play or strategy, so that the game form advantages a set of running patterns and ball movement is not new (Wade, 1967). Often the approaches come out of different traditions. For example, Richard Light has explained the Game Sense approach from the perspective of complex learning theory (Light, 2013). A constraints-led approach emerged from dynamic systems theory (Davids et al., 2008) and Newell's (1986) constraints framework while TGfU emerged initially as a teaching model for secondary physical education (Bunker & Thorpe, 1982). There has been some work done showing the pedagogical similarities between instruction assumptions in Game Sense approach and a constraints-led approach (Breed & Spittle, 2011; Pill, 2014). I agree with Breed and Spittle (2011) who suggested that game-based approaches have in common playing a game as the central organisational feature of a session. The games create conditions that emphasise certain playing features in order to develop player understanding.

DUNCAN: To be honest, I often think that the pragmatics of good coaching get lost in arguing for the benefits of one model over another. If I go into State league level there is a fair bit of game-based coaching, but if I go into community coaching at training there are many drills. At State league you get a better selection of coaches, more people who have invested in their coach education and have developed their understanding of coaching by going to coach education and conferences. They are able to have conversations with other elite coaches and they are exposed to more coaching concepts, and they see more examples of game-based coaching. Whereas at community level, they are not full time in coaching, and outside of hours their time is spent coaching. They are not going to conferences, spending time around experienced high performance coaches, and involved in coaching conversations during the day. They are plumbing, or teaching or nursing during the day. You can have the coaching knowledge from going to the coach accreditation, but unless you are involved in the ongoing conversations, you only get the general idea and your coaching does not substantially change. Your coaching practice reflects your experience and coaching knowledge.

CHERIE: There is certainly something to that. I remember an Australian football research piece where the coach explained that his first introduction to game-based coaching was attending a coach accreditation course. He had never experienced it as a player at amateur league or in his coaching apprenticeship prior to doing the course (Pill, 2015).

DUNCAN: I read some work recently about the role of deliberate practice in developing sport expertise. How does a game-based approach fit with deliberate practice?

CHERIE: Andres Ericsson used the term 'deliberate practice' to describe the focused, structured, detailed and continuing practice at 'getting better'. Deliberate coaching practice involves activities that are used for the purpose of improving players. In game-based coaching, players participate in an environment deliberately designed by the coach for a learning purpose (Pill, 2017). In my opinion, game-based coaching fits the description of deliberate practice if: (1) the challenge point of the game provides stretch where players are pushed to the boundary of their comfort zone in order to create the conditions for learning; (2) the game has specific, well-defined learning intentions; (3) there is effort on behalf of the players to focus on the defined learning intentions; (4) there is high quality feedback in the form of questioning and cueing by coaches, and (5) players develop a mental representation of expertise (Ericsson & Pool, 2016).

DUNCAN: I recently worked with a coach I thought was good. I found the coach good at designing activities and conditioning the game using constraints to establish starting points for the players. Good on strategy, the coach had identified the need to teach players to not take the ball out of defence the way that it came in, to change lanes by 'going in one way and out the other'. This is an example where the coach 'gets' the principles of play, but they are weak on coaching player tactical responses and therefore the system breaks down for them, and they do not understand why the players can't execute good decision making in the game.

CHERIE: In a way, I am not surprised. Using questions to develop thinking players is the area of game-based coaching that many coaches struggle with, and yet it is perhaps this pedagogical aspect of game-based coaching that makes it player-centred (Zuccolo, Spittle & Pill, 2013, 2014). We possibly don't pay enough attention to this in our workshops.

DUNCAN: Thanks for the chat, but I need to press on with some other work. Can we catch-up again later in the week to finalise our presentations so we are 'singing from the same song sheet'?

CHERIE: Sure. I will email you a calendar invite.

The coaches depart the café for their cars.

Conclusion

The conversation between the coach educators highlights the tension between the concern researchers and academics have with theory generation and explanation, and adherence to tenets of a model, and coaches as theoretically informed but concerned with the situational reality of their context as coaches. Stolz and Pill (2016) referred to this as the interpretative pragmatics that takes place in coaches making these theoretical models work for them. In a sense, academics and coach educators may have to concern themselves with the theoretical foundations of the practical endeavour of coaching to justify certain viewpoints on practice design. It may however be more realistic to expect coaches to engage thoughtfully with theory and models while putting themselves into practice rather than putting theory into practice (Collins, 1991).

Green's (2000a) concept of the everyday philosophy of the practitioner can help to understand the theory-practice divide that can occur in the natural setting of the coaching context, where the coach theoretically informed puts their self into the practice of coaching. This involves the coach putting into practice an amalgamation of theory from coach education and 'taken for granted' beliefs and practices from their experience of coaching – their practical knowledge. Many coaches are therefore in a state of 'becoming' formed in their coaching practice as they inherit and continue to hold certain beliefs about what 'good coaching' is despite alternative ideas being put before them in coach education. In continuing to hold these beliefs, coaches demonstrate a high level of commitment and limited detachment to their philosophy of coaching (Elias, 1987). This is a position that can prevent coaches from accepting more reality adequate or less 'mythical' ways of coaching – such as adopting the evidence informed ideas of game-based coaching informed by recognised theoretical positions. This means that coach pedagogical and experiential knowledge provides an orientation to the instructional task of coaching at practice, which reflects their personal and situated context rather than a fixed idea or model of coaching (Green, 1998, 2000a, 2002). Coaches knowledge can thus be considered as understandably lying on a continuum of greater or lesser adequacy or alignment with the tenets of game-based coaching, but never 'truly' aligned or fully formed and in alignment in an absolutism sense (Green, 2000b; Harvey & Pill, 2019).

References

Armour, K. (2006). The way to a teacher's heart: Narrative research in physical education. In D.Kirk, D.Macdonald & M. O'Sullivan (eds), *The handbook of physical education* (pp. 467–485). London: Sage.

Australian Sports Commission. (1996). *Game sense: Perceptions and actions.* Research report. Canberra, ACT: Australian Sports Commission.
Breed, R. & Spittle, M. (2011). *Developing game sense through tactical learning: A resource for teachers and coaches.* Melbourne, Vic: Cambridge University Press.
Bunker, D. & Thorpe, R. (1982). A model for the teaching of games in secondary schools. *Bulletin of Physical Education,* 18(1), 5–8.
Charlesworth, R. (1994). Designer games. *Sport Coach,* 17(4), 30–33.
Charlesworth, R. (2016). *World's best: Coaching with the Kookaburras and the Hockeyroos.* Nedlands, Western Australia: RC Sports.
Coffee, D. & den Duyn, N. (1997). *Game sense: Developing thinking players* (video). Belconnen, ACT: Australian Sports Commission.
Collins, M. (1991). *Adult education as vocation: A critical role of the adult educator.* New York: Routledge.
Davids, K., Button, C. & Bennett, S. (2008). *Dynamics of skill acquisition: A constraints-led approach.* Champaign, IL: Human Kinetics.
Elias, N. (1987). *Involvement and detachment.* Oxford: Basil Blackwell.
Ericsson, A. & Pool, R. (2016). *Peak: Secrets from the new science of expertise.* Boston, MA: Houghton Mifflin Harcourt.
Green, K. (1998). Philosophies, ideologies and the practices of physical education. *Sport, Education and Society,* 3(2), 125–143.
Green, K. (2000a). Exploring the everyday 'philosophies' of physical education teachers from a sociological perspective. *Sport, Education and Society,* 5(2), 109–129.
Green, K. (2000b). *Philosophies, ideologies and the practice of physical education: Making sense of the everyday 'philosophies' of physical education teachers from a sociological perspective.* Leicester: University of Leicester.
Green, K. (2002). Physical education teachers in theory figurations: A sociological analysis of everyday 'philosophies'. *Sport, Education and Society,* 7(1), 65–83.
Greenwood, R. (2019). Eddie's wonder goal shows practice makes perfect: Tex. *The Advertiser,* 24 April.
Gréhaigne, J. F., Wallian, N. & Godbout, P. (2005). Tactical-decision learning model and students' practices. *Physical Education and Sport Pedagogy,* 10, 255–269.
Harvey, S. & Pill, S. (2019). Exploring physical education teachers 'everyday understandings' of physical literacy. *Sport, Education and Society,* 24, 841–854.
Jones, R. (2006). *The sports coach as educator: Reconceptualising sports coaching.* London: Routledge.
Jones, R. (2007). Coaching redefined: An everyday pedagogical endeavour. *Sport, Education and Society,* 12(2), 159–173.
Light, R. (2013). *Game sense: Pedagogy for performance, participation and enjoyment.* New York: Routledge.
Metzler, M. (2011). *Instructional models for physical education* (3rd ed.). Scottsdale, AZ: Holcomb Hathaway.

Mosston, M. & Ashworth, S. (2002). *Teaching physical education*. San Francisco, CA: Pearson Education.

Newell, K. M. (1986). Constraints on the development of coordination. In M. G. Wade & H. T. A. Whiting (eds), *Motor development in children: Aspects of coordination and control* (pp. 341–360). Dordrecht, Netherlands: Martinus Nijhoff.

Pill, S. (2012). *Play with purpose: Developing game sense in AFL footballers*. Hindmarsh, SA: ACHPER Publications.

Pill, S. (2014). Informing Game Sense pedagogy with constraints led theory for coaching in Australian football. *Sports Coaching Review*, 3(1), 46–62.

Pill, S. (2015). Implementing game sense coaching approach in Australian football through action research. *Agora for Physical Education and Sport*, 18(1), 1–19.

Pill, S. (2017). The Game Sense approach as explicit teaching and deliberate practice. In J.Williams (ed.), *Proceedings of the 30th ACHPER International Conference*, Canberra, Australia, 16–18 January, 133–145.

Pill, S. (2019). The game sense approach: Developing thinking players. *Runner: The Journal of the Health & Physical Education Council of the Alberta Teachers' Association*, 49(1), 32–39.

Pill, S. & SueSee, B. (2020). Developing the game sense approach as play with purpose. In S.Pill (ed.), *Perspectives on game-based coaching* (pp. xx–xx). New York: Routledge.

Renshaw, I., Davids, K., Newcombe, D. & Roberts, W. (2019). *The constraints-led approach: Principles for sports coaching and practice design*. New York: Routledge.

Stolz, S. & Pill, S. (2014). Teaching games and sport for understanding: Exploring and reconsidering its relevance in physical education. *European Physical Education Review*, 20(1), 36–71.

Stolz, S. & Pill, S. (2016). A narrative approach to exploring TGfU-GS. *Sport Education and Society*, 21(2), 239–261.

Tinning, R. (2010). *Pedagogy and human movement: Theory, practice, research*. London: Routledge.

Viciana, J. & Mayorga-Vega, D. (2014). Differences between tactical/technical models of coaching and experience on the instructions given by youth soccer coaches during competition. *Journal of Physical Education and Sport*, 14(1), 3–11.

Wade, A. (1967). *The FA guide to training and coaching*. London: The Football Association.

Wein, H. (2004). *Developing game intelligence in soccer*. Spring City, PA: Reedswain.

Worthington, E. (1974). *Teaching soccer skills*. UK: Lepus Books.

Zuccolo, A., Spittle, M. & Pill, S. (2013). Twenty years of Game sense sport coaching in Australia: 1993–2013- where are we now? *In Proceedings of the 28th ACHPER International Conference*, 27–29 November, Melbourne (pp. 188–196).

Zuccolo, A., Spittle, M. & Pill, S. (2014). *Game sense research in coaching: Findings and reflections*. University of Sydney Papers in HMHCE, 15–30.

12 Coaches' use of game-based approaches in team sports

Donna O'Connor, Paul Larkin and Oliver Höner

Team sport coaches play a major role in a player's acquisition of the skills necessary for successful performance (Ford, Yates & Williams, 2010). They are seen as teachers, and the behaviours and activities they use create a meaningful learning environment (Ford et al., 2010; Partington & Cushion, 2013) in order to convey important concepts for the development of the player's technical and tactical skills (Cushion & Jones, 2001; O'Connor & Larkin, 2015; O'Connor, Larkin & Williams, 2017). This can be achieved by building and managing a positive learning environment, whereby specific performance-based objectives can be accomplished. Pedagogical researchers believe one of the best methods to do this is via a game-based approach (Bunker & Thorpe, 1982; den Duyn, 1997; Kidman, 2005; Pill, 2012, 2014; Roberts, 2011). A game-based approach (GBA) promotes a player-centred learning environment, whereby the coach focuses on activities such as small-sided games, while attempting to use fewer instructions. The coach needs to allow players to problem solve and take responsibility for their own learning within an environment which replicates the demands of the game (O'Connor & Larkin, 2015).

Team sport players are required to perceive and respond to the continuous flow of stimulus from the game environment for effective performance (Davids, Renshaw & Glazier, 2005). The premise of small-sided games is to recreate the competitive environment, whereby the interaction between players are constantly changing in a dynamic manner creating opportunities to challenge the player whilst efficiently performing sport-specific technical skills (Davids, Araújo, Correia & Vilar, 2013). This use of small-sided games to recreate the competitive environment replicates movement constraints (i.e. opposition), information variables from the specific environments, and the functional coupling between perception and action processes from competition (Pinder et al., 2011). Therefore, a small-sided game can improve performance by providing a holistic integrated approach that is high in representation to match-play, and allows for the components of team sport performance (i.e. technical skills, tactical awareness, physiological and psychological attributes) to be applied within the one activity (Bonney et al., 2019; Hill-Haas, Dawson, Impellizzeri & Coutts, 2011; Davids et al. 2013). Representation to match-play is achieved by incorporating interpersonal interactions from competitive performance, including the coordination tendencies between a player or group of players and the environment (Davids, et al., 2013). By manipulating the game environment players are given the opportunity to interpret game-related cues, explore options, apply tactical strategies, make decisions, and execute technical skills, while experimenting with their decision making and skill execution within a game-related environment (Hill-Haas et al. 2011; O'Connor, Wardak, Goodyear, Larkin & Williams, 2018).

GBA from an activity sense

A key component of a GBA is how coaches create activities which promote player learning. Generally, when describing the learning environment, researchers differentiate between game-based activities (i.e. similar to the full version of the sport, such as small-sided modified games) and drill-based activities (i.e. do not replicate the full version of the sport, such as technique drills with no opponents; Ford & O'Connor, 2019). The reason for this differentiation is that practice activities that replicate the full version of the sport contribute to the acquisition of technical and tactical skills, whereas, drill-based activities may primarily focus on technical skill development (Ford et al., 2010; O'Connor et al., 2017; Partington & Cushion, 2013; Partington, Cushion & Harvey, 2014).

To assess the coaching environment, researchers use systematic observation tools to monitor the time invested in game-based and drill-based activities. Early investigations found a general consensus that team sport youth coaches invested a larger proportion of practice time in drill-based activities (56–69%) compared to game-based activities (19–47%) (Ford et al., 2010; Low et al., 2013; Partington & Cushion, 2013; Partington et al., 2014). These results suggest that despite the proposition that game-based activities provide greater opportunities for player development there is a gap between research evidence and applied coaching (Ford et al., 2010). There has however, been a recent shift in team sport coaching practice, with researchers finding a greater percentage of time invested in game-based (41–63%) compared to drill-based activities (20–22%) (Ford & Whelan, 2016; O'Connor et al., 2017). This shift may be a result of increased awareness of GBA benefits and changes to coach education programmes.

GBA from a coaching behaviour perspective

In addition to the practice activities, another key component of the team sport learning environment is the instructional behaviours used by coaches (Ford et al., 2010). Despite contemporary researchers indicating best practice coaching behaviours (Cushion, Ford & Williams, 2012; Harvey, Cushion & Massa-Gonzalez, 2010; Kidman, 2005), generally coaches emulate other coaches, resulting in a learning environment shaped by the use of established, traditional or coach-centred approaches, characterised by a direct and prescriptive approach (Cushion et al., 2012; Ford et al., 2010; Partington & Cushion, 2013; Partington et al., 2014). This direct and prescriptive approach is reinforced by the coach observation literature, which indicates the most frequently used coach behaviour is instruction, with questioning, especially divergent questions (i.e. questions with the potential for multiple responses), used sparingly within practice sessions (Cushion & Jones, 2001; Ford et al., 2010; Partington & Cushion, 2013). While a coach-centred approach may provide the coach with a notion of control over the session and an impression of a more effective use of time (O'Connor, 2012), an issue associated with constant instruction is the potential for lower skill retention and performance decrements under pressure, such as competitive performance environments (Masters, 1992; Raab, 2003).

To overcome these limitations of the coach-centred approach, pedagogical researchers suggest inquiry-based approaches, such as a GBA (Bunker & Thorpe, 1982; den Duyn, 1997; Kidman, 2005; Pill, 2012, 2014; Roberts, 2011) are more effective. A GBA affords structure and facilitates learning through player-centred environments, whereby the individual's interaction within the learning environment fosters understanding and problem solving (Harvey et al., 2010; Kidman, 2005; Partington & Cushion, 2013). Therefore, the challenge for a coach is to reduce the amount of direct instruction while guiding players to discover solutions to sport-specific problems, using questions, prompts and feedback (Kidman, 2005). This coach behaviour strategy enhances player learning by stimulating players to engage in higher order thinking (Harvey et al., 2010; Partington & Cushion, 2013). For example, this may be achieved by creating situations where players analyse information (i.e. the activity or cues), create solutions, and then evaluate their outcomes.

While coaches are increasingly aware of GBAs, researchers have investigated whether this knowledge translates into practice. Partington and Cushion (2013) interviewed coaches following observation of their practice sessions. The interview data indicated that the coaches would create learning environments to promote player development with questioning being proposed as the main pedagogical strategy. However, evident from the practice session observation, there was limited use of questions. This finding demonstrates that while coaches are aware of the importance of questioning for creating effective player learning environments, there is a disconnect between intention and practice (Harvey et al., 2010; Roberts, 2011). As such, coaches may be utilising a GBA, but still over coach (i.e. providing frequent concurrent instruction to tell players what to do) and limit the potential effectiveness of this type of approach for player learning. Thus, while research findings may demonstrate coach's awareness of the associated benefits for GBAs, there is still more work to be done in educating them in the specific strategies associated with this style of learning.

Strategies coaches use to incorporate GBA's into their sessions

Coaches need to have the professional knowledge of their sport to consider the technical, tactical and physiological demands of their sport when incorporating a GBA. How they creatively manipulate game constraints such as rules, number of players, field dimensions and time will influence the opportunities players have to execute and make decisions. From a cognitive perspective, the aim of the game or problem posed allows players to read the situational cues, make decisions on and off the ball, and trial different strategies so they gain a better understanding of time, space and risk (O'Connor & Larkin, 2015). From a motivational perspective, coaches are encouraged to consider the needs of their players to create a learning environment that promotes high levels of enjoyment, motivation, engagement and autonomy (Hornig et al., 2016).

Overall, coaches have an opportunity to be innovative in their design of game-like activities as they endeavour to develop decision making (Miller et al., 2017; O'Connor et al., 2017), tactical awareness (Chatzopoulos, Drakou, Kotzamanidou & Tsorbatzoudis, 2006; Light & Robert, 2010), technical skill execution (Klusemann, Pyne, Foster & Drinkwater, 2012), and physiological development (Hoffman, Reed, Leiting, Chiang & Stone, 2014). Findings have demonstrated incorporating more game-based activities (90%) over a nine week period resulted in players' decision making and support play during 4 versus 4 netball improve at a greater rate than players participating in more drill-based activities (<40% game-based) over the same time period (Miller et al., 2017). Therefore, demonstrating the potential impact of this approach to coaching.

In a recent study where elite football coaches were asked to conceptualise how they develop player decision making they outlined pedagogical approaches such as playing with others; effective communication; balancing structure and autonomy; knowledgeable inspiration from other players and coaches; and a focus on improvement rather than winning (O'Connor et al., 2018). Each of these conceptions can inform game-based coaching and the effectiveness of the practice environment as they highlight the importance of planning, the use of 'the right kind of questions … that make the players think' (p. 268), being careful of 'over coaching is killing creativity' (p. 268), and creating activities that 'give the players the freedom to make the right decisions themselves' (p. 268).

Elite rugby coaches have also shown that they value a GBA at training to develop match specific fitness, decision making and game awareness, and test players' skills in game situations (Light & Robert, 2010). Coaches in this study highlighted the importance of implicit learning, although they varied in their level of player autonomy (e.g. emphasising structure and limited options), and all thought questioning should be left to the conclusion of the game and wasn't an integral part of player learning (Light & Robert, 2010). O'Connor and colleagues (2017) extended this finding by examining the learning environments coaches created to specifically develop decision making in football players. Coaches indicated they wanted to create small-sided games based on real game scenarios that provided opportunities for repetition; use questioning, guide decision-making by providing cues and solutions; and manipulate the game constraints to promote quick thinking and decision-making opportunities. Observations of the sessions revealed all 29 youth coaches devised a game-based activity with coaches utilising possession, target player, multiple goals or 1 versus 1 games. The majority of coaches used uneven teams of less than 5 players. Interestingly, these different constraints did not alter the number of on-ball decisions made, while most actions (e.g. first touch, passes, running with the ball, evade opponent) were executed at a high success rate (>85%). The coaches' behaviour during the activity was stop–start to enable them to instruct and ask questions. For example, coaches allowed players to participate for 130 seconds followed by 85 seconds of inactivity (i.e. player listening to the coach). This was repeated six to seven times during the activity with approx. 5 seconds of concurrent instruction occurring every 20 seconds of activity, and an average of one question asked per minute (e.g. where is the space? What can you do to help him get free?). The authors concluded that although the youth coaches were aware of strategies that may promote decision making opportunities by implementing game-based coaching, there was a tendency to over-coach, and the stop-start nature of practice with coach interruptions limited the problem-solving opportunities of players (O'Connor et al., 2017).

Although there is limited evidence that game-based coaching is superior to drill-based coaching for developing technical skills (Chatzopoulos et al., 2006; Miller et al., 2017) there is also no evidence to suggest that technical skill development is impeded through the use of games (Kinnerk, Harvey, MacDonncha & Lyons, 2018). However, coaches generally adopt game-based coaching for its holistic development of players rather than a focus on one specific performance element. Coaches incorporate small-sided games into their sessions as it places players in a competitive environment where manipulating field dimensions, player numbers, rules and duration influence the physiological, technical and tactical demands placed on players (Klusemann et al., 2012; Bonney et al., 2019). During these small-sided games, players are learning implicitly as they react and adapt to the unpredictable and variable conditions, have more skills opportunities and work with their team mates to problem solve under pressure and fatigue (Davids et al., 2013).

Challenges

Game-based coaching can present several challenges for coaches when first adopting this approach. These include: having the knowledge of the game to firstly identify tactical problems, and then creating a game-based activity that reflects this problem so players can devise solutions through guided discovery (Thomas, Morgan & Mesquita, 2013); manipulating constraints to better align with goals (O'Connor et al., 2017); finding the balance between short term goals (e.g. winning on the weekend) and longer-term player development (e.g. focus on learning) (Mckay & O'Connor, 2018); adopting a more facilitative coaching role (Thomas et al., 2013); not having enough time or losing patience, so coaches feel they have to jump in and 'tell' players (Light & Robert, 2010; Thomas et al., 2013); and knowing when and how to use questions (O'Connor et al., 2017; Roberts, 2011; Thomas et al., 2013). To assist in the transition to game-based coaching, coaches may benefit from: filming their practice to assist with self-reflection; having a 'critical friend' observe practice; support from a mentor; and attending coach development workshops.

Conclusion

Implications and recommendations for practice

Time invested in the planning stage is important for coaches adopting a GBA. They need to identify their area of focus or problem from the game. Being clear on the learning goal will assist in designing an activity that provides numerous opportunities for players to respond and adapt to the environment as they move towards the desired outcome. Coaches need to consider the knowledge and skill level of their players as they determine 'what' and 'how' to manipulate the task (e.g. space, time, rules, equipment). This will allow coaches to keep players in the 'challenge' learning zone (i.e. just out of their comfort zone where players are stretched).

Further, coaches should plan questions and potential teachable moments to ensure they are intervening at appropriate times and potentially reducing the prescriptive nature of the session. This planning and clear focus on the intended learning goal will assist coaches to understand how the athletes may respond to the activity and enable them to consider appropriate responses to athletes' potential problems in achieving the learning goals. For example, coaches should consider when to interrupt (level of mistake or timepoint in the activity); and how to act (ask questions, provide instruction, give praise, modify activity).

Players need to see the link (or be directed towards the link) between the modified games and 'real' game. Therefore, coaches need to consider how representative the activity is in relation to the movement patterns and perception-action couplings of the competitive environment.

Coaches may be tempted to stop the activity too frequently – expect some 'messiness'. Give players time to experiment, make mistakes, and correct their own errors. Adopt a facilitative approach and use questions and cues to guide and shape player actions rather than dictate what they should do. Players should be actively engaged in their learning and all have an opportunity to practice and receive feedback.

In certain situations, coaches may consider also incorporating other activities (e.g. drill-based) to assist athlete learning (e.g. for a specific skill deficiency).

Future research

As coaches aim to improve complex and holistic phenomena like the development of players and their actions, game-based activities seem to be an appropriate practical approach for coaching in team sports. However, further research is needed on a theoretical as well as empirical level to provide a clearer understanding and more evidence for GBA's. Comprehensive and interdisciplinary theories of coaching are needed that integrate concepts from different disciplines: e.g. motivational psychology, motor and cognitive learning, and training science (high intensity training). Although more holistic theories are necessary to frame complex phenomena like coaching players' action and learning processes, the empirical analyses and evaluation of these 'broad' theoretical concepts is a challenge. For example, for studies evaluating GBAs regarding their effectiveness in promoting the intended outcomes (e.g. decision-making, motivational climate, sustainable skill development) demanding research designs are needed (e.g. in regard to duration, control group design, sample size, matched skill levels, retention tests, reporting validation procedures of the intervention, inclusion of objective measurements to supplement qualitative data) and multiple moderator variables or circumstances that might change the results must be considered (e.g. different ages, performance levels, communities, sports).

References

Bonney, N., Berry, J., Ball, K. & Larkin, P. (2019). Australian Football skill-based assessments: A proposed model for future research. *Frontiers in Psychology*, 26 February. Retrieved from https://doi.org/10.3389/fpsyg.2019.00429.

Bunker, D. & Thorpe, R. (1982). A model for the teaching of games in secondary schools. *Bulletin of Physical Education*, 18(1), 5–8.

Chatzopoulos, D., Drakou, A., Kotzamanidou, M. & Tsorbatzoudis, H. (2006). Girls' soccer performance and motivation: Games vs technique approach. *Perceptual and Motor Skills*, 103(2), 463–470.

Cushion, C. J. & Jones, R. L. (2001). A systematic observation of professional top-level youth soccer coaches. *Journal of Sport Behavior*, 24(4), 354–376.

Cushion, C., Ford, P. R. & Williams, A. M. (2012). Coach behaviours and practice structures in youth soccer: Implications for talent development. *Journal of Sports Sciences*, 30(15), 1631–1641.

Davids, K., Renshaw, I. & Glazier, P. (2005). Movement models from sports reveal fundamental insights into coordination processes. *Exercise and Sport Sciences Reviews*, 33(1), 36–42.

Davids, K., Araújo, D., Correia, V. & Vilar, L. (2013). How small-sided and conditioned games enhance acquisition of movement and decision-making skills. *Exercise and Sport Sciences Reviews*, 41(3), 154–161.

den Duyn, N. (1997). *Game Sense: Developing thinking players*. Canberra, Australia: Australian Sports Commission.

Ford, P. R. & O'Connor, D. (2019). Practice and sports activities in the acquisition of anticipation and decision-making. In A. M. Williams & R. C. Jackson (eds), *Anticipation and decision-making in Sport* (pp. 269–285). London: Routledge.

Ford, P. R. & Whelan, J. (2016). Practice activities during coaching sessions in elite youth football and their effect on skill acquisition. In W. Allison, A. Abraham & A. Cale (eds), *Advances in coach education and development: From research to practice* (pp. 112–123). London: Routledge.

Ford, P. R., Yates, I. & Williams, A. M. (2010). An analysis of practice activities and instructional behaviours used by youth soccer coaches during practice: Exploring the link between science and application. *Journal of Sports Sciences*, 28, 483–495.

Harvey, S., Cushion, C. J. & Massa-Gonzalez, A. N. (2010). Learning a new method: Teaching Games for Understanding in the coaches' eyes. *Physical Education & Sport Pedagogy*, 15(4), 361–382.

Hill-Haas, S. V., Dawson, B., Impellizzeri, F. M. & Coutts, A. J. (2011). Physiology of small- sided games training in football. *Sports Medicine*, 41(3), 199–220.

Hoffman, J., Reed, J., Leiting, K., Chiang, C. & Stone, M. (2014). Repeated sprints, high-intensity interval training, small-sided games: Theory and application to field sports. *International Journal of Sports Physiology and Performance*, 9(2), 352–357.

Hornig, M., Aust, F. & Gullich, A. (2016). Practice and play in the development of German top- level professional football players. *European Journal of Sport Science*, 16(1), 96–105.

Kidman, L. (2005). *Athlete-centred coaching: Developing inspired and inspiring people.* Christchurch, NZ: Innovative Print Communications.

Kinnerk, P., Harvey, S., MacDonncha, C. & Lyons, M. (2018). A review of the game-based approaches to coaching literature in competitive team sport settings. *Quest*, 70(4), 401–418.

Klusemann, M., Pyne, D. B., Foster, C. & Drinkwater, E. (2012). Optimising technical skills and physical loading in small-sided basketball games. *Journal of Sports Sciences*, 30(14), 1463–1471.

Light, R. & Robert, J. E. (2010). The impact of Game Sense pedagogy on Australian rugby coaches' practice: A question of pedagogy. *Physical Education and Sport Pedagogy*, 15, 103–115.

Low, J., Williams, A. M., McRobert, A. P. & Ford, P. R. (2013). The microstructure of team practice activities engaged in by elite and recreational youth cricket players in England. *Journal of Sports Sciences*, 31, 1242–1250.

Masters, R. S. W. (1992). Knowledge, knerves and know-how: The role of explicit versus implicit knowledge in the breakdown of a complex motor skill under pressure. *British Journal of Psychology*, 83(3), 343–358.

Mckay, J. & O'Connor, D. (2018). Practicing unstructured play in team sports: A rugby union example. *International Sport Coaching Journal*, 5, 273–280.

Miller, A., Harvey, S., Morley, D., Nemes, R., Janes, M. & Eather, N. (2017). Exposing athletes to playing form activity: outcomes of a randomised control trial among community netball teams using a game-centred approach. *Journal of Sports Sciences*, 35(18), 1846–1857.

O'Connor, D. (2012). Challenges facing Youth Coaches. In J. O'Dea (ed.), *Current issues and controversies in school and community health, sport and physical education* (pp. 283–294). New York: Nova Science.

O'Connor, D. & Larkin, P. (2015). Decision-making and tactical knowledge, an Australian perspective to their development in youth players. In T. Favero, B. Drust & B. Dawson (eds), *International research in science and soccer II* (pp. 204–214). London: Routledge.

O'Connor, D., Larkin, P. & Williams, A. (2017). What learning environments help improve decision-making? *Physical Education and Sport Pedagogy*, 22(6), 647–660.

O'Connor, D., Larkin, P. & Williams, A. M. (2018). Observations of youth football training: How do coaches structure training sessions for player development? *Journal of Sports Sciences*, 36(1), 39–47.

O'Connor, D., Wardak, D., Goodyear, P., Larkin, P. & Williams, M. (2018). Conceptualising decision-making and its development: a phenomenographic analysis. *Science and Medicine in Football*, 2(4), 261–271.

Partington, M. & Cushion, C. (2013). An investigation of the practice activities and coaching behaviors of professional top-level youth soccer coaches. *Scandinavian Journal of Medicine and Science in Sports*, 23, 374–382.

Partington, M., Cushion, C. & Harvey, S. (2014). An investigation of the effect of athletes' age on the coaching behaviours of professional top-level youth soccer coaches. *Journal of Sports Sciences*, 32, 403–414.

Pill, S. (2012). Teaching game sense in soccer. *Journal of Physical Education, Recreation and Dance*, 83, 42–52.

Pill, S. (2014). Informing Game Sense pedagogy with constraints led theory for coaching in Australian football. *Sports Coaching Review*, 3, 46–62.

Pinder, R. A., Davids, K., Renshaw, I. & Araújo, D. (2011). Representative learning design and functionality of research and practice in sport. *Journal of Sport and Exercise Psychology*, 33(1), 146–155.

Raab, M. (2003). Decision-making in sports: Influence of complexity on implicit and explicit learning. *International Journal of Sport & Exercise Psychology*, 1(4), 310–337.

Roberts, S. J. (2011). Teaching games for understanding: The difficulties and challenges experienced by participation cricket coaches. *Physical Education and Sport Pedagogy*, 16(1), 33–48.

Thomas, G., Morgan, K. & Mesquita, I. (2013). Examining the implementation of a teaching games for understanding approach in junior rugby using a reflective practice design. *Sports Coaching Review*, 2, 49–60.

Index

action fantasy games 40
actualising tendency 37, 42
affective 96; concept 72; dimension 50; domain 73, 74, 75; learning domain 41, 70, 72; Learning Design (ALD) 40, 45; richness 86
affordances xxii, xxiii,
Almond, Len 49
assessing student learning 69
assessment 69, 71, 73, 74, 75; of conditions 47, 52; formative 74; information 71; of performance 7; of players 16; procedure 70; process 70; purpose 70; qualitative 88; of risk xxiii
athlete-centred xxiv, 38, 82, 103
athletics 60, 62
athlete learning 123
Australian football 58, 59, 60, 61, 62, 112
Australian Football League (AFL) xii, xxiv, 57, 58, 62, 63, 64
Australian Sports Commission xvii, xxiii, xxiv, 2, 4, 5, 96, 97, 102, 108, 110
autonomy 37, 38, 120, 121

badminton xxv, 67, 68, 69, 73, 74, 75
baseball 23, 24, 26, 32, 33, 34, 35, 41,
basketball xxiv, 13, 19, 42, 45, 46, 47, 49, 52, 54, 60, 61, 63, 86, 91
batter 15, 24, 26, 28, 29, 30, 32, 33, 34
Batty, Eric xvii

behaviourist xxi, 2
Bourdieu', Pierre 65
bowling 47, 51,
boxing 60
Brooking, Trevor xvii
Bruner, Jerome 12, 49

challenge point xxiii,17, 113,
CHANGE IT 102
Charlesworth, Rick 4, 41, 110
clinics 68
Clinic Game-Day model 68, 69
coach-centred 119
coach educator xxv, xxvi, 108, 109, 114
coaching artefact xxv, 93
cognition xxi, 12, 13, 41
cognitive 2, 8; activities 13; artefacts 89; capabilities 48; domain 70, 71; engagement 25; framework xxii; lens xxi; orientation xxi; operation 6; opportunities 21; psychology 41; stage 93
Command Style 4, 97
common content knowledge (CCK) 80
Complex learning theory 112
conditioned games xix
constraints xxii, 6, 38, 39, 62, 63, 81, 84, 91, 109, 110, 113, 121, 122; approach xxii; framework 112
constraints-led xxii; xxiii, 102, 111, 112
constructivist learning theory 70
Convergent Discovery Style 6, 7

Index

corporeal artefacts 89,
counter-factual xxiv, 40
coupling 117
cricket xxiv, 13, 18, 42, 45, 47, 48, 51, 60, 61, 62
cueing 113

decision-making xviii, xxiv, 4, 5, 23, 24, 26, 28, 30, 32, 33, 41, 47, 82, 83, 86, 88, 92, 93, 96, 97, 109, 121, 124
debate 70, 92, 109; of ideas xxi, 100
Deleplace, René xvii
deliberate design 1,2, 3, 5, 102
deliberate play 62,
deliberate practice 3, 6, 113
design features 12
Designer games xxiii, 4, 40, 45, 97, 110
Developing Thinking Players (DTP)
Differentiated 101; differentiate 117
Digital Video Games Approach (DVGA) 11, 14, 16, 18, 19
Digital video game design xxiv, 11
discovery barrier 1
discussion 25, 33, 38, 41, 57, 64, 70, 79, 80, 83, 109
direct instruction xvii, 3, 67, 96, 97, 119
Divergent Discovery Style 6, 7
divergent questions 119
drill 2, 3, 5, 68, 69, 93, 110, 112; drill-based 109, 118, 119, 121, 122, 123

early specialisation 65
efficiency index 71, 73
eliminate 102; elimination 102,
elite players 86, 87
embodied cognition 36
environment constraints 102
epistemological xxiii, 36, 39, 86; epistemologies 58
Ericsson, Andres 113
exaggerate 102, 103; exaggeration 102
Existentialism 36, 37, 38
expertise 3, 58, 60, 61, 62, 64, 65, 113

facilitate 57, 80, 84, 88, 93; facilitator 77, 82, 92

feedback 3, 5, 6, 16, 69, 74, 97, 103, 112, 119, 123
fielder 15, 24, 27, 28, 29, 30, 32, 33
formative assessments 74
freeze replay xix

game categories 14, 15, 74
game constraints 120, 121
game design 11; game design theory xxiv; game design method 4; deliberate xix
game form xxiii, 4, 45 61, 64, 65, 68, 71, 110, 111, 112
Game Intelligence model xxiii, 108, 112
Game Insight model xxiii
game model 45, 46, 47, 48, 49, 51, 54, 68, 70
game modification 3, 4, 97, 102
game learning 81; game-based learning 82, 83
Game Sense xxiii, 21, 36; approach xvii, xxiv, 1, 2, 5, 96, 99, 100, 101, 102, 103, 104, 105, 108, 112; coaching xvii, 2, 83, 93, 111; model 99, 101; pedagogy xxv, 83; player game sense 81, 109
game play xvii, xix, xxii, 2, 3, 4, 5, 12, 13, 17, 20, 21, 78, 80, 98, 103, 109; performance 73
game understanding xxiv, 3, 4, 11, 17, 20, 102
Gee, James Paul 11, 12, 14
goalkeeper 78, 79, 82; goalkeeping 79
Good Digital Game Design model 12, 14, 15
Grehaigne, Jean-Francois xvii, xx, xxi
Greenwood, Ron xvii
Guidance 3,14, 20, 53, 97
Guided Discovery Style 7, 97

Heidegger, Martin 36
Hughes, Charles xvii
Humanism 36, 37

Immersive Game-based Narratives (IGNs) 40, 41, 42, 45, 50, 51, 55
improvised games 65
Indigenous Australians 57

informal games 57, 62, 63, 64;
  training 64, 65
inquiry 1, 57, 109; inquiry-based
  approaches 119
instrumental theory 90, 93
Intrinsic Motivation Inventory 70
invasion games 17, 46, 70

Kierkegaard, Soren 37

learn xxi, xxv, 7, 25, 46, 61, 63, 74,
  77, 83, 84, 87, 93, 97
learner xxii, xxiv, 4, 6, 7, 12, 15, 50,
  70, 84, 92, 93, 101
learning xxii, xxvi, 3, 4, 7, 12,
  13, 14, 16, 21, 23, 24, 40, 41,
  49, 50, 57, 59, 59, 62, 64, 65, 67,
  68, 69, 74, 75, 77, 81, 82, 86, 87,
  92, 97, 100, 103, 113, 119, 120,
  121, 122, 123, 124; activities 92;
  coherence 111; contexts 65;
  design 45; dimensions 51;
  domains 103; environment xxv, 1,
  93, 117, 118, 119, 120, 121;
  episode 8; experience 81; goal 123;
  intention, 110, 113; needs 102;
  perspective 69; process 13, 25, 96,
  124; purpose 113; strategies 13, 14;
  tasks 80; theory 70; tool 75;
  zone 123
linear 2,

Mahlo, Friedrich xvii, xxi
match practice xviii
material artefacts 89
mental representation 3, 86, 112
metacognition 11, 13, 14, 20, 83
modifications 3, 4, 23, 97, 98, 101,
  102
modified games 1, 27, 29, 31, 50, 62,
  68, 110, 118, 123
modify 26, 69, 102, 103; activity 123;
  equipment 24; games 102;
  instruction 82; modifying 4
Mosston, Muska 5, 97, 111
motivation xx, 14, 24, 25, 60, 62, 65,
  72, 97, 120, 124
motivational psychology 124
motor skills xx, 88
movement constraint 117

National Rugby League (NRL) xxiv,
  57, 58, 63, 64
net-wall games 69, 70, 73, 74
non-linear 2, 101; pedagogy 41;
  process 14

ontological 40, 42
open drill 2, 5, 111
optimum learning 65

pedagogy xix, xxv, xxvi, 2, 4, 7, 8, 23,
  41, 57, 65, 82, 83, 84
Pedagogical Content Knowledge
  (PCK) 81
Perception xxii, xxv, 13, 50, 73, 89,
  93, 117
perception-action coupling 123
performance standards 7
Phenomenology 38, 45
phenomenological 35, 36, 39; ideas 50;
  lens 40; method 38, 39; project 40,
  42; principles 42; research 39, 40
physical literacy 2
pickleball 69, 74
player learning 11, 108, 121
Play Practice xxiii
Play with purpose xxiii, 1, 3, 4, 8, 99,
  101, 103, 104, 105
player learning xxi, 20, 24, 117, 118
Positive pedagogy 45
practice games xxii
Practice Style 5, 6, 7, 8, 97, 105
principles of play xviii, xix, xxii, 12,
  110, 113
problem solving xxiv, 1, 12, 13, 14,
  15, 63, 66, 83, 97, 100, 119, 122
proficiency 24, 88, 90, 93
procedural knowledge 12, 70
production (discovery) cluster 6, 7
psychomotor domain 70;
  developments 74; skills 73

question 2, 6, 7, 25, 30, 32, 37,
  39, 41, 45, 47, 52, 58, 70, 72, 75,
  78, 80 81, 82, 83, 90, 93, 98, 100,
  101, 113, 119, 120, 121, 122, 123
questioning 1, 20, 25, 67, 82, 83, 100,
  113, 119, 120, 121; protocol 83;
  purposeful 100
questionnaire 97

Redknapp, Harry xvii
reflect 24, 32, 37, 67, 71, 83, 100, 101, 109, 112, 114, 122; reflecting 7, 20, 75, 86; reflection xxvi, 2, 6, 38, 62, 63, 70, 73, 105; reflective 1, 20, 100
regulatory artefacts 89
replicate 40, 117, 118; replication xvii, xxv, 2, 97
representation 3, 14, 50, 60, 86, 89, 90, 100, 113, 118
representative xxii, 50, 96, 97, 100, 101, 123; activities xxv, 97; design xxii, 3; nature 40; teams 63; representiveness 45
reproduction cluster 4, 6
Rogers, Carl 37

self-reflection 122
Self Teaching Style 4
SeeSaw tool 70, 71, 73, 75,
shape play 81; shape player actions 123; shaping play 84
shortstop 26, 27, 28, 29, 30
simplifying 4; simplification 102
situated learning 65
skill acquisition 109, 111
skill drills 110
skill development 24, 61, 64, 74, 118, 122, 124
skill learning xx
small sided games xviii, 82, 117, 121, 122
softball 23, 24, 26, 27, 29, 31, 32, 33, 34
soccer xviii, xxiii, xxiv, xxv, 11, 17, 61, 62, 64, 72, 75, 77, 78, 79, 80, 81, 83, 84
specialised content knowledge 80
Spectrum of Teaching Styles/ The Spectrum 1, 4, 5, 6, 7, 8, 97
strategy xx, 2, 15, 55, 74, 79, 83, 102, 110, 112, 113, 119, 120

student learning data 67
systems of play xviii, xx

tactical apprenticeship 92
Tactical Decision Learning Model 108
Tactical Games Model 112
tactical principles 12
tactics xxviii, 7, 23, 24, 26, 30, 32, 34, 37, 79, 80, 86
task constraint 6
teachable moment 100, 123
team-centred 38
Teaching Games for Understanding (TGfU) xxiii, xxiv, 21, 23, 36, 45, 49, 50, 67, 68, 111, 112
Team Sport Assessment Procedure (TSAP) 69, 70, 71, 73, 74, 75
technical knowledge 89
technique drills 118
technological approach 88, 90
tennis xx, xxii, 69, 70, 74, 96–105
thinking players xvii, xxiv, 1, 2, 3, 8, 23, 26, 27, 29, 31, 96, 113
time constraint 13
Tomlinson, Carol Ann 101
toolkit xxv, 1, 8, 81, 97, 98, 110, 111
transfer of learning 3

understanding: deep 12, 13, 14, 45; game xxiv, 4, 11, 17, 20, 102; strategic 11, 12, 17, 20; tactical xxiv, 12, 23, 24, 26, 32, 62

Verbal Protocol Analysis Procedure 71
Volleyball 34, 69, 74, 83, 89, 91
Vygotski, Lev xxv, 90, 92, 93

Wacquant, Loïc 65
Wade, Allen xvii, 110
Wein, Horst 108
Winterbottom, Walter xvii
Worthington, Eric xvii

For Product Safety Concerns and Information please contact our EU representative GPSR@taylorandfrancis.com
Taylor & Francis Verlag GmbH, Kaufingerstraße 24, 80331 München, Germany

www.ingramcontent.com/pod-product-compliance
Lightning Source LLC
Chambersburg PA
CBHW051749230426
43670CB00012B/2212